SHORT STORY MYSTERIES

WITH A WESTERN FLAVOR

By

Loy Ann Bell

To Sherry -
Many hours of happy
reading to you.
Love,
Loy Ann

Everyone loves a good horse race. The photo on - the cover illustrates the story, "Easy Lovin'", which starts on page 69 and is set in the fabulous world of Quarter Horse racing.

Most of the stories in this book are fiction. Names, characters, places, and incidents are products of the author's imagination or are used fictitiously and are not to be construed as real. Any resemblance to actual events, locales, organizations, or persons, living or dead, is entirely coincidental. Two stories are exceptions—Johnny Jump-up and Murder, Unadulterated are creative nonfiction, while Bobby Jones and Taylor Brown actually did enter The Wild Cow Milking, but the story is fictional except for the ending, which happened the way I told it.

Lab Publications
1285 So. Lincoln Ave., Apt. #2
Jerome, Idaho 83338
www.lan_paints@yahoo.com

Copyright © 2012 by Loy Ann Bell

ISBN: 978-0-9857122-0-4

All rights reserved. No part of this book may be used or reproduced in any manner whatsoever without written permission, except in the case of brief quotations embodied in critical articles and reviews. For more information, address Lab Publications.

Printed in the United States of America

For Bobby Jones

I dedicate this book to the memory of my dear friend, Bobby Jones. He was the older brother I never had, and from the time I was three years old, he told the best "windies" I've ever heard.

By the way, these stories were written with a western flavor in mind, and not correct English. Rest assured, I do know the difference.

Additional books may be ordered from Amazon.com.

I would like to thank Linda Mecham of the Jerome Public Library, and the girls from Copy-It, Twin Falls, for their assistance in publishing this book. I wouldn't have made it without them. My thanks also to my "readers" who either read my manuscripts and offered candid opinions and advice or listened while I read the stories aloud so I could act as "my own worst critic": Margaret Hays, Yvonne Szajgecki, Corrine McDowell, Carol Sterrett, Louise Lampman, Norma Fiscus, Vivian Volkers, Dave Gray, Rick Barnes, and Donya Brown. And of course, the members of our Writers' League Critique Group from the Twin Falls Chapter have proved invaluable: Bill Strange, Vaughn Phelps, Loyd Bakewell, Evonne Biggins, Gary Rasmussen, Bernice Richardson, Loraine Fischer, and Pat Walch. The stories wouldn't have been "perfected" without your help.

My sincere gratitude to Mrs. Joe Jolicoeur of New Mexico, Lisa Zebarth, Marta Loveland, Caldwell, Mrs. Steinley of Steinley Photography of Coeur d' Alene, Andrea Jensen of Thatcher, Idaho, Jay Pitcher of Smithfield, Utah, Linda Giltner and Karen Daniels of Jerome, Les Bois Park of Boise, and Marsha Christiansen Renund of Heber City, Utah for assisting me in my search to locate the right racing photo for the cover of my book. I first wrote the story about a Palomino colt, but found one black race horse among some 10,000 photos where the jockey's colors matched the trappings on the horse. So I rewrote the story for a black horse…

SHORT STORY MYSTERIES
WITH A WESTERN FLAVOR

Table of Contents

The Atlanta Accident	Page	1
The Brown Recluse	Page	15
Premeditated Revenge	Page	35
The Fight	Page	55
Easy Lovin'	Page	69
Johnny Jump-up	Page	83
Strike Four, You're Dead	Page	99
The Wild Cow Milking	Page	121
Stymied	Page	135
Murder, Unadulterated	Page	155

SHORT STORY MYSTERIES

"The Atlanta Accident" was the first short story I ever wrote. I entered it in the 2006 Idaho Magazine Fiction Contest and won second place! I was elated, and the award encouraged me to write more short stories.

The Atlanta Accident

In May, 1952, the inhabitants of Atlanta, Idaho were leaving like rats off a sinking ship. The mines were nearly depleted of gold and Atlanta was fast becoming a ghost town. Boards already covered the windows of the school. Most of the small homes were deserted, particularly the ones with wooden sides and floors and tents draped over them.

My new bride, Gloria, and I parked in front of Charlie's Place, a combination bar/café/and grocery store. Relieved to stretch our cramped legs after the six-hour, seventy-six mile trip, we climbed out of the car and sauntered inside.

LOY ANN BELL

A short, grizzled bartender and a grubby, bearded miner were perched on bar stools talking. The miner wore a soiled faded blue work shirt and a battered, old gray hat.

We sat down a couple of stools away.

"What kin I do fer ya?" the bartender asked.

"I'd like a glass of tea," I said.

"And I'd like a Coke, please." Gloria's silky blonde hair bobbed as she looked around.

The bartender yelled into the café, "Corrine, fix us some tea, will you?"

He reached for a Coke, opened it, and set it on the bar in front of Gloria. "Where're you folks from?"

"Fairfield," I replied.

He nodded. "Been there. Which road did you take to get here?"

"We came from Mountain Home through Rocky Bar."

"It took us over six hours." Gloria sighed.

"You're lucky you even got through this time of year," said the bartender. "In the summer when the road's dry, you can make it in a little over three hours. But it's actually faster to go around by Boise, even though it's longer. What brings you to Atlanta?"

"We've never seen the old town. And I'd like to find my uncle. Do you know Walter

SHORT STORY MYSTERIES

Woodell?'

The bartender nodded. "Yeah, but you're outta luck. The Talache Corporation owns another big mine in Sandpoint and he went to work up there a year ago."

"Darn." My voice reflected my intense disappointment.

A round-faced, gray haired woman walked in and set my glass of tea in front of me. "There you go, dearie," she said with a smile. She returned to the café.

Just then the door flew open and slammed into the wall with a loud bang. A well-muscled, six-foot guy with a crew-cut swaggered to the bar. A yellow Lab-cross, square-headed dog followed. I pegged the guy as ex-Marine. At first glance, the dog appeared ferocious, but when he saw us, he wagged his tail and trotted over. After getting acquainted, he wandered back and plopped down at his owner's feet.

"I wanna a Draft, Charlie. Now." The guy had a voice that sounded like grating gravel.

Charlie hustled to grab a glass, draw a beer, and set it in front of the ex-Marine. Reaching over the bar, the man clamped a huge fist around a knot of fabric in the little bartender's shirt collar. "You know I don't like a buncha foam on my beer,

Charlie," he growled.

Nearly choking from air constriction, the little bartender mumbled, "Okay, Mr. Morton."

If I read the Marine correctly, he would have enjoyed belting someone half his size. He shoved as he let go Charlie's collar, and the bartender fell back into the liquor bottles. Charlie righted himself. "I'll get you another one." His hands shook as he drew another beer.

I couldn't see any foam on the first beer and took an instant dislike to Morton.

The bully emptied both glasses and stalked out the door without paying for them, his dog trotting behind.

The little bartender sighed with relief and walked back to where we sat.

"Ya oughta shoot that no-good bastard," the miner said.

"It is tempting," Charlie replied.

After a moment, the miner turned to me. "Hey, you wanna a job?"

"How much does it pay?" I asked in a smart-aleck voice. I was making eighty cents to a dollar an hour as a farmhand in Fairfield.

"Buck forty an hour," he stated. "And you actually only work seven hours a shift 'cause it takes an hour to get to and from the diggins'. But you get paid for eight."

SHORT STORY MYSTERIES

I lost my cockiness and got real interested.

"The Talache Mine here in Atlanta is down to a skeleton crew, but I'm still finding enough gold to make it pay, and I need a mucker."

"What's a 'mucker' do?"

"You'd help me set the drill, dynamite, and fuses. After blasting, you use the little donkey engine that runs the bucket on the cable to scoop out the rubble and dump it three hundred feet down a chute into ore cars on the main level. There's not much work with picks and shovels." He tipped his hat back on his head and took a swig of beer.

"I'll take it!" The extra money would allow me to buy a better car since my black 1948 Frazier had quit me a few times. Suddenly I remembered I'd gotten married and hadn't consulted Gloria. I glanced at her. She looked horrified. "That is, if my wife agrees," I amended.

"But where would we live?" she asked, her eyes wide.

"Quite a few houses are vacant since so many people have left town." The miner climbed off his stool. "Come 'mere." He led the way to the door, opened it, and pointed at a little house up the street. "The guy who owns that one told somebody yesterday he'd rent it for twelve bucks a month. Let's finish our drinks, and go look at it." We walked back to the bar and emptied our glasses.

"By the way, my name's Walt Maguire." We shook hands, and the three of us headed for the door.

Our footsteps sounded hollow on the board sidewalks, then made peculiar sucking noises as we walked up the muddy street.

Intrigued with the little town, I asked, "How many people live here now?"

"There are about twenty families left."

Most of the houses had been "thrown up" overnight and weren't built very well. Although small, the house Walt showed us had a substantial wood foundation, a small kitchen, living room, and bedroom. An outhouse stood in the backyard.

"It even has electricity," Maguire said.

"Electricity?" I asked, surprised.

"Atlanta has its own power plant," he explained.

At first Gloria protested, but the extra money finally convinced her that we should take advantage of the opportunity. "We do need another car," she admitted. "The Frazier isn't very reliable."

"You'd best buy groceries when you go home to get your stuff 'cause groceries are high here," my new employer advised. "But if you need it, Charlie's wife, Corrine, fixes great lunches. In fact, she makes the best elk roast sandwiches I ever ate."

My wife and I had a long drive ahead of us; we planned to get our business taken care of and be back by Tuesday night. Since Gloria probably wouldn't have time to unpack and get the kitchen organized, I stopped and ordered a sack lunch from Corrine for the following Wednesday.

"I went into Boise a couple of days ago so I've got dill pickles, green onions, potato chips, carrot slices, celery sticks, and apples," she said, smiling. "What would you like?"

I made my selections.

"I'll fix it and have it ready by seven thirty on Wednesday morning," she promised. "What's your name so I can write it on your sack?"

"Jim Woodell," I replied.

Gloria and I drove back to Fairfield, hurriedly packed our belongings, and returned by Tuesday night.

At seven forty-five the next morning, I went into Charlie's to pick up my lunch. Twenty-two brown sacks labeled with names sat on the counter. I pawed through them until I found mine, paid Corrine, and went on to work. At noon, the elk roast sandwich tasted as delicious as Walt Maguire had predicted.

LOY ANN BELL

Standing five-eight and heavyset, my new boss walked like his feet weighed two hundred pounds apiece. I couldn't determine his age since only his prominent nose showed—the beard and mustache obscured the lower part of his face and his old, soiled hat drooped down over his eyes. Walt turned out to be a pretty decent guy.

During the first week I lived in Atlanta, I arrived at two conclusions. First, the whole town was a melting pot of misfits. Every person seemed unique, a character in his or her own right. Second, miners are all a little nuts and have no sense of humor. They're always a foot away from a million dollars; they never find it, but they keep looking. And they always think someone is trying to jump their claims—using legal or illegal methods.

Walt and I usually stopped at Charlie's and had an after-shift drink each day at 4:30 when we finished working in the mine.

Charlie Short, aptly named because of his five-foot-five height, owned the bar and cafe. In his late fifties, he walked with a limp, clipped his words when he talked, and constantly spouted jokes. His wife, Corrine, twice his size, appeared to be at least ten years younger, pudgy, and constantly wore a smile. And boy, could that woman cook! She and Charlie seemed to get along quite well except when he got a snoot full of his own merchandise. Then

SHORT STORY MYSTERIES

Corrine lost her patience and her smile.

Another character, Wayne Desmond, looked to be about thirty-two and he was long—long bodied, long faced, and long nosed. He worked in a mine, but he could play a guitar quite skillfully. Did we ever hit it off! Eager to learn, I grabbed my old guitar and tried to learn all the licks that he could teach me. We spent many evenings serenading the neighbors.

It was Wayne who introduced me to the brothers, Bill and Dave Hanford, as we drank an after-shift drink in the bar one day. In his late forties, Bill had shaggy, dark brown hair and bushy eyebrows. His brother, Dave, was probably at least ten years younger and a couple inches taller with black hair and the same square face. He was handsome in a seedy sort of way.

A couple of weeks later, after I'd become acquainted with the brothers, we were sitting in Charlie's when a miner in dire need of a shave and a bath came in and spoke to Dave. They moved a few feet away. Wayne, Bill, and I continued to talk, but I noticed Bill kept one eye tuned towards the miner and Dave's conversation. Bill suddenly jumped up and yelled, "Don't sell! He's trying to cheat you."

I surmised that the miner wanted to buy

some equipment from Dave who'd evidently been about to sell.

"Butt out," the miner growled at Bill.

Like a streak, Bill leaped over the table and pinned the rank-smelling man against the wall. An old rusty knife appeared from nowhere and dug into the guy's throat. Blood dripped.

"Don't tell me to butt out," Bill snarled. "Dave is my brother and you're trying to cheat him."

When he let the miner up, the guy ran for the door and didn't look back.

Right then, I came to the conclusion that Bill had probably looked out for his younger brother all his life.

Although cautious around them after that episode, I liked the brothers. Bill called me "kid." I listened, spellbound, to their wild, fascinating tales about mining in Mexico. They'd fought many battles and probably won most of them because Mexican miners didn't like gringos, especially gringos who infringed on Mexican mining territory. In fact, most gringos not only didn't return with gold; they didn't return at all. But I noticed the brothers were able to buy whatever they needed, and figured they had gold stashed.

As the brothers and I sat in Charlie's on another hot afternoon, the ex-Marine, Morton, swaggered in, his dog padding along behind. He ordered a beer, but this time he didn't pick on Charlie.

"That's Cleo Morton," Bill said softly. "Too bad he hasn't got a personality like his dog. I like Sam."

The dog made the rounds. After Charlie petted him, he headed over to us and Bill reached down and stroked the dog on the head. "How're ya doin', Sam?" Sam wagged his tail.

Charlie set a beer on the bar. Morton took a swig, looked around to see where the dog had gone and noticed him at our table. "Get over here, Sam," he commanded.

Sam sent us a remorseful look, but moseyed over to his owner and lay down. Until then I had doubted if Morton treated the dog well, but I saw him feed Sam some popcorn from a bowl on the bar, so I changed my assumption.

"That one's a tough character," Bill said quietly.

"He sure worked *me* over one time." Dave fished in his pocket for a nail clipper and began cleaning his nails. "Blindsided me."

To me, Morton appeared to be all brawn and no brains. "Hope he's smarter than he looks," I commented.

"Dumber'n a post!" Bill's voice had a steel edge to it. "And he likes to fight."

"That's for sure." Dave agreed. "I asked a gal to go to dinner with me. That's what made 'im mad. Hell, I didn't even know he had dubs on her."

Bill shook his head. "Steer clear of that one, kid."

I had no problem taking his advice; regardless of how Morton treated his dog, in my estimation, the guy was still an S.O.B.

Every so often, I got a craving for another of Corrine's delicious elk sandwiches, so I'd stop and order one for the next day.

One night, Wayne Desmond walked over to my house, his guitar case in hand. He set it down. "Did ya hear about Cleo Morton?"

"The Marine?"

"Yeah. He's been sick with stomach pains and vomiting the last few days. They think he drank some water that had arsenic in it. Anyway, that's what the symptoms indicated. He went into convulsions and died last night."

"No kidding!" Morton's image popped into my mind. The big, overgrown Marine had seemed invincible.

"The idiot musta been a ways from town, got thirsty, and drank some water from a stream." Wayne frowned. "He shoulda known better."

"I thought all miners knew that arsenic is a by-product of mining," I said. "Walt warned me the first day I came to work about drinking the water from any streams close to town because when gold, silver, or zinc is separated from the rest of the ore, arsenic is one of the elements that's flushed away with the water."

"That's right," Wayne agreed. "Everybody knows that streams close to mining areas are usually contaminated with arsenic."

I made up my mind to be darned careful where I drank water from then on.

The next morning when I told my boss, the news about Morton he exclaimed, "Good riddance!"

Naturally, Morton's death caused a buzzing in the small town. I hadn't ever officially met the guy, so I shed no tears, but no one else seemed broken up over him either. In fact, they seemed relieved. Charlie went to the funeral; I think he just wanted to make sure Morton wouldn't be bullying him anymore. Anyway, he reported that only a handful of people even attended and after a week, the buzzing died down.

* * *

That memorable summer I learned a lot about mining and actually enjoyed the work. I saved enough money to buy a newer 1951 metallic silver blue Ford coupe, which made Gloria very happy.

Stopping by the brothers' camp one day, I talked to Bill for a few minutes before I noticed that Dave wasn't there.

"Where's Dave?" I asked.

"Went to the store." Bill fished a file out of his toolbox and, bracing his shovel between his legs, began sharpening it. "He'll be back directly."

We discussed the weather and Atlanta's depleting mines. Finally I said, "You know, Morton's death bothers me. But I guess the big dummy got thirsty and figured he was far enough away from the mines, the water would be safe." I shook my head. "Stupid. And his dog died too—with the same symptoms."

Bill stopped filing, looked up at me from under his bushy eyebrows. "That's not the way it happened, kid. The arsenic was in the sandwich." He shook his head sadly. "I felt bad about the dog."

SHORT STORY MYSTERIES

Many times spouses do not understand the love or passionate commitment that horse people often have for their horses. I took this fiction story to extremes, although I have known two very vain women in my lifetime that might have reacted as Darla did in this story. In 2006 "The Brown Recluse" won the $1,000 Author Mania Short Story Contest in Texas.

THE BROWN RECLUSE

Darla stood before the full-length mirror in her black lace bra and panties.

"I'm a knockout," she said aloud, admiring her honey blonde hair—she went twice a week to the beauty salon to have it styled, colored, or permed. She held out her dainty hands, then glanced down at her toes—regular manicures and pedicures enhanced her pretty hands and feet. Her hour-glass body was perfectly shaped—she bought a yearly membership to the health club, worked out daily, and attended aerobics classes three times a week, so her legs were shapely. The skin on her lovely face appeared rosy and unblemished—she spent a small fortune on L'Oreal products to keep her skin beautiful. She kept three charge cards active buying the latest designer clothes to show off her figure. And of course, it was only fitting that a woman as gorgeous as she should drive a late model Cadillac.

And does my husband appreciate my exhaustive efforts? she fumed. *Is he attentive to my needs? No, he's usually outside in the corral, grooming and talking to his stupid horse. Why do I, when I look like a movie star, have to play second fiddle to a black Quarter Horse stallion?*

"My husband doesn't pay enough attention to *me*, but if anyone mentions that damned horse, he nearly pops his shirt buttons, can't wait to take them out to see Ebony," she muttered. "In fact, he carries five different poses of that dumb horse in his wallet, but only one of me. It makes me sick."

Sex doesn't seem to interest him anymore. Not that I like sex all that much, but otherwise, how can I maintain leverage over him? Besides, I need to feel wanted and desired, don't I?

I could have had any man I wanted. What did I ever see in John anyway? She considered that question. First, he had money and after all, she required money to keep herself looking great—the health club membership, charge cards, etc. And he did buy her a new Caddy every other year. Second, he stood six-foot-two with light brown hair and blue eyes set in an attractive face. That's why she'd married him. How could she have known he would become infatuated with a blooming horse? Oh, how she hated the creature.

One day, since the small town they lived in didn't have a bookstore, Darla drove to Barnes & Noble in Twin Falls. She found the mystery section and began searching for the latest Sue Grafton novel. Feeling eyes upon her, she noticed a tall, dark haired man staring at her. Used to men admiring her, she now expected it. *Why shouldn't he stare at me? I'm gorgeous,* she thought. She turned first one way, then another, to make sure he could see all sides of her luscious figure, then smiled demurely at him.

Immediately he walked over and said, "I'm sorry. I didn't mean to stare at you, but you are so beautiful."

He'd told her exactly what she wanted, what she deserved to hear. "Why, thank you," she said. "Are you from Twin Falls?"

"Yes, I teach Biology at the high school. My name is Eric Martin and you're....."

"Darla Stanfield." She could tell by his dark, smoldering eyes that he wanted her. *I need to feel desired after the rejection I've been getting at home,* she reasoned. *I need to be held, to be loved. I deserve it. My husband doesn't care what I do; all he cares about is that damned black horse.* She smiled at Eric Martin again.

"How 'bout a cup of coffee?" he asked.

She didn't want to seem too eager. "Well....."

"Come on, we can go over to the Rancho." He nodded at the restaurant across the street.

"All right," she replied. The Rancho wasn't as snazzy as she liked, but she'd overlook that for the moment.

Her three-inch, red, stiletto heels tapped a cadence on the pavement as they walked.

Inside, the lunch crowd had dwindled to a half dozen people and Darla didn't see anyone she knew. Relief washed over her. She couldn't have some ignorant tattletale running back and reporting to her husband, although she felt confident he'd believe whatever she told him.

Eric's words were flattering, but his voice sounded sincere and his eyes worshiped her.

Within an hour, she went to see his apartment, knowing full well what would happen. She walked in, didn't even have time to inspect the premises before he spun her around, and began kissing her, wildly, passionately.

"Where have you been all my life, doll?" he

mumbled between kisses. In his haste, he started to tear her clothes off, but of course, her expensive clothing was far more important to her than sex with him.

"Take it easy," she cautioned. "You're going to rip my blouse."

Which only made him want her all the more. But he managed to suppress his lust and carefully, though hastily, undid the buttons, leaving the blouse intact.

They made love the rest of the afternoon. His sexual appetite seemed insatiable; he couldn't get enough of her.

She had him right where she wanted him—in her power. Exhilaration surged through her; she felt like a woman again.

The clock in his living room chimed seven times and brought her back to reality with a jolt. She had to get home. Dressing hurriedly, she grabbed her purse and headed for the door.

"When will I see you again?" he asked urgently. "At least let me have your phone number."

Knowing she would be the only person to answer her cell phone, she gave him the number, ran out, climbed into her blue Caddy and drove off before he could kiss her goodbye.

She'd barely walked into the house when Eric Martin called. "Hi, doll, when I can see you again?"

Glancing out the window, she saw John brushing the stallion in the corral.

"I could come to Twin tomorrow afternoon," she said softly.

"Great! What time? Do you remember how to get to my apartment?"

Smiling, she said. "Of course. I'll be there by 1:00." And she hung up.

The next afternoon passed quickly for them. This time, Eric wouldn't let her leave until he'd extracted her promise that she'd return the following day.

During the next month she slipped away every chance she could. She knew Eric had fallen totally, desperately in love with her and before long, he began to pressure her to marry him.

"I love you, doll. Get a divorce and marry me," he said.

But he didn't have any money so, of course, she couldn't do that. She tantalized him but managed to skirt the issue by never giving him a straight answer.

At home, Darla's jealousy of the horse escalated. She considered killing the despicable creature, but soon discarded that idea—the stallion had monetary value. And, after all, money was money.

One morning her husband, John, came home from the doctor's office, a bag in his hand. "I have diabetes," he announced as he set the bag on the table. "Have to watch my diet and check my blood often 'cause my kidneys are failing. Doc says I'll probably have to take dialysis treatments before long." If he expected sympathy, he didn't get it.

She hadn't known he'd even been to see the doctor. It suddenly occurred to her that he looked *old*.

Pulling the paraphernalia from the bag, he showed her how it worked—as if she cared. *Well, he isn't going to drag me down with him. I'm not ready to die yet. I'll divorce him.* In the middle of his explanation, she made an excuse and hurried from the room.

The next day she called for an appointment with a Twin Falls lawyer. She couldn't consult the hometown attorney; John might find out.

"Anthony Briswell, Attorney at Law" said the black, gold-engraved sign that hung beside the door of the long, brown, modern building. Darla walked into the plush, beige-carpeted waiting room. An older woman sat typing on a computer keyboard. Her gray hair was pulled back severely into a bun, and the bifocal lines in her metal-framed glasses showed plainly. Darla viewed her with disdain. The years had claimed the woman; she had no class at all.

"Mrs. Stanfield?" the secretary asked.

"Yes," Darla said, looking everywhere but at the woman.

"Mr. Briswell is expecting you." The secretary rose, showed Darla into the inner office, and quietly closed the door on her way out.

The lawyer, fiftyish and stout, had dressed in a brown suit with gleaming shoes to match and his dark hair had been neatly trimmed. He stood, extended his hand, introduced himself and waved her to the chair across from his desk.

"What can I do for you?" he asked.

"I want a divorce," she announced.

The lawyer pulled out a pen and yellow legal pad from the desk drawer. "Does your husband beat you? Step out on you?"

"No," Darla said. "I have to play second fiddle to a blooming horse!"

Briswell looked up, suppressed a grin. "I'm not sure a judge will consider that grounds for a divorce."

That was not what she wanted to hear. "Just tell me what my rights are," she said impatiently.

He studied her.

"When I sue him for divorce, can I get half of everything he owns?"

"I don't know what you and your husband have, but whatever you've accumulated since you married him, you're entitled to half."

"We've been married seven years," she said. "He already owned the ranch when I met him."

"In that case, if he didn't mortgage the property after you were married, it's his." He glanced at her questioningly.

She shook her head. "No, he didn't mortgage it."

"What have you acquired since you've been together?"

"My car and his pickup," she replied. "We haven't needed anything else."

"Both paid for?" the lawyer asked.

"Yes."

"Then, depending upon the value of each, you'd probably be awarded your car and he'd get his pickup. Unless he bought equipment to run the ranch."

"Nothing else?" She couldn't believe it.

He shook his head firmly.

"He already had all the equipment he needed to run the place," she said thoughtfully.

"Then your car is probably all you are

legally entitled to."

"I'm going to be left out in the cold," she wailed.

The attorney looked at the ceiling, then scrutinized her intently. "Oh, come now," he said. "A woman as attractive as you will never be left out in the cold."

Her eyes spit fire as she jumped up. "You're no help whatsoever. What do I owe you anyway?" She intended to pay cash so no bill would be sent to her home.

"Nothing," he replied. "I don't charge for a consultation."

She stormed out of the office, slamming the door. It dawned on her before she'd driven two blocks. She couldn't get anything except her car if she divorced John. But he had no children, so if he died, she would inherit everything—the ranch, the equipment, the livestock, the house, his pickup, even the damned horse. She considered all the ramifications.

Driving straight to Eric's apartment, she quickly enticed him into bed, and responded to his lovemaking more passionately than usual. Afterward, she lay in his arms, picking at the curly, dark hairs on his chest.

"Are you going to marry me or not?" he demanded.

SHORT STORY MYSTERIES

"I just consulted an attorney," she said. "I can't divorce John or I'll lose everything."

"There has to be a way."

"I'll just have to wait until he dies," she said carefully. "Then I inherit it all. God only knows I deserve it after putting up with that silly horse for so long."

"But he could last thirty years," Eric protested.

"I don't think so. He's now a diabetic." She looked at him calculatingly.

"So?"

"So the doctor told him his kidneys are failing. He will probably need dialysis treatments before long."

"He could still live several years," Eric said.

"Not if his kidneys fail."

Eric sat up, stared at her, taking the bait just as she'd planned. "So we figure out how to make his kidneys fail." After a moment, his eyes gleamed. "How about a spider bite? That would look like an accident."

"A spider? Yuck. I hate spiders." She wrinkled her nose in distaste.

He rose, went to his computer, turned it on, and typed "poisonous spiders" in the search box.

Scanning down the list that appeared on the

screen, he highlighted one. "A brown recluse ought to do the job. See? This is what one looks like."

Darla followed, cringed when she saw the awful looking spider on the monitor. It had a beige-colored violin on its back, the legs were hairy, and it reminded her of a picture of a demon she had once seen.

Oblivious to her reaction, Eric continued. "A bite kills the cells and literally eats the flesh. The skin turns from red to a purplish color, and an ulcer forms. Like this." He pointed to a photo of a hideous-looking lesion.

The color drained from her face as she looked at the horrible sight.

"Like I said, the bite can cause kidney failure," he added.

She forgot her repugnance. "And he already has weak kidneys. What an ingenious way to kill him!"

"A spider bite won't kill him immediately. It might take awhile. Just don't rush him to a doctor. The longer you wait, the better."

She nodded. "I understand."

"Be sure you take out life insurance on him beforehand," he said.

"Oh, we took out life insurance policies several years ago. One million dollars apiece. It's a good thing we did. No preexisting kidney problems then." She thought a moment. "But can you find one of those spiders?"

"I'm a biology teacher, remember? I know where they live."

She smiled.

The next day at Eric's apartment, he welcomed her with a kiss, and dug in a desk drawer. "I captured a brown recluse." Triumphantly, he held up a small round glass jar.

She peered at the ugly creature crawling inside. "Oooh, what a terrible looking thing!"

Eric grinned. "He is. You must remember he's aggressive and can jump as far as five feet, so be very careful when you turn him loose."

"I'll put him in bed while John's asleep. He'll never know what happened."

"Tonight?" Eric took her in his arms, kissed her passionately. "I want to make you mine, baby. The sooner the better."

"Yes, I'll do it tonight." She gingerly picked up the jar and cringed at the arachnid which stared venomously back at her. She put the jar inside a plastic bag so she wouldn't have to look at it while she drove home.

John's pickup was gone when she pulled in the driveway so she had no problem sneaking the spider into the house and hiding it behind some sweaters stacked on a shelf in her walk-in closet.

An hour later, her husband arrived, tired and hungry. After a quick dinner, he showered, donned his pajamas, and sat down to watch TV. Darla began counting the minutes until bedtime. It seemed an eternity before he decided to turn in. She shut the TV off and followed. He climbed into bed and turned over, his back to her. Thirty minutes passed before she heard him snoring. To be safe, she waited another thirty minutes before folding the covers back, rising, and tiptoeing to the closet. Shutting the door before turning the light on, she retrieved the little round jar. The brown recluse gazed at her. She shivered. What a mugly-ugly creature.

Flipping the light switch off before opening the closet door, she tiptoed back to the bed, and carefully unscrewed the lid. Again she listened for John's steady breathing. Holding the lid, she placed the jar upside down on the bed and shook the spider out close to his blue-striped, pajama-clad back then quickly pulled the covers up. Nothing to do now but wait. When he moved or turned over, the spider would bite him. A surge of ecstasy raced through her. Only a matter of time until she owned everything. And $1,000,000 to spend however she wished.

John would soon be dead. Eric didn't know

it, but when she no longer needed him, she meant to send him packing. He wouldn't dare talk to the authorities because of his involvement in the crime. For sure, she didn't need his help to spend a million dollars. She'd find someone in her class, her league, someone with oodles of money. Eric didn't measure up to husband status because he only earned a teacher's paltry wages.

Taking the jar to the kitchen, she washed it thoroughly in hot, soapy water, mixed herself a screwdriver, and turned the TV on. But she couldn't concentrate on the program, and kept wondering what was happening in the bedroom. Forcing herself to sip the drink slowly until at last she couldn't stand the suspense any longer, she tiptoed back to the bedroom. Had the spider bitten John yet?

She studied her husband's body lying among the covers. *His chest is not moving! He's not breathing. But where's the spider?* Fear gripped her, but if she pulled the covers back to hunt for the spider, it might bite her. *I've got to get the thing out of the bed. But how?* She finally decided not to chance looking for it and called 911. "It's my husband. I don't think he's breathing," she told the dispatcher. "Send somebody quick!"

Soon she heard a siren screaming, getting

louder and louder as it drew nearer. The ambulance stopped in front of the house. She opened the door, and led the two EMT's to the master bedroom.

One felt John's carotid artery for a pulse and shook his head.

Darla deserved an Oscar for her convincing performance. "But how? And why?" she cried.

The other EMT ran to call the police.

Within minutes other sirens sounded, and two Sheriff's cars pulled in the driveway, then four deputies swarmed through the house.

Darla began wailing loudly. An EMT finally gave her a shot, mainly to shut her up.

She awoke to an antiseptic odor in a small, sunny, white-walled hospital room. "Where am I?" she mumbled. Then she noticed the salt and pepper haired, middle-aged man sitting in the chair next to the bed. He wore a conservative gray suit with a geometric-designed gray and gold tie.

"You're in the Twin Falls Hospital, Mrs. Stanfield."

Memories of the night before flooded her mind. This man looked like a cop, so she'd have to be careful what she said. "Is John okay?"

"I'm sorry to have to tell you this, ma'am, but your husband is gone."

"Gone? What do you mean gone?"

"He's dead."

"Dead? But how?"

"Funny thing. We found a brown recluse spider in the bed. They're deadly, you know. I would suggest you have your house sprayed because there may be more of them around."

"He died from a spider bite?"

"Actually, no. He committed suicide."

She jerked upright. "Committed suicide?"

"Yes. He left a suicide note. When you're better, you can read it."

"I want to read it now," she said.

"Well, if you think you're up to it….." He picked up his briefcase, opened it, took out a piece of paper, and handed it to her. She recognized John's legible handwriting.

Dear Darla,

My health is deteriorating. I have no living relatives, and I'm quite sure you will not care for me in my illness. You're the most vain, self-centered person I've ever had the misfortune to know.

Therefore, I am taking the easy way out—with an overdose of insulin. You will not be able to collect the $1,000,000 life insurance policy since there is a clause that states no money will be paid in *a case of suicide.*

My lawyer drew up another will three days ago while you were off playing around with your boyfriend in Twin Falls. The house, the ranch, and all my other possessions, I'm leaving to Ebony. He has brought me a great deal of joy in my loneliness.

You may reside at the ranch as long as you are single, but no boyfriends will be allowed on the place. If you remarry, you will, of course, vacate the premises immediately.

These conditions are contingent upon Ebony remaining alive and well. If something should happen to him, all my worldly possessions will be sold and the proceeds donated to the American Diabetes Association. I have appointed a friend who will monitor the horse's well being.

Your car is yours to keep and I have provided a reasonable, monthly allowance. If you are frugal, you will be able to live on it.

Your husband,
John

Darla grabbed a glass of water from the hospital roll-around stand and threw it. The plastic water glass bounced off the wall and clattered across the floor while the water dripped downward, staining the wall a dirty gray color.

"That dirty, conniving SOB. How dare he leave me penniless!" she screamed.

The blue-tinged profanity that followed, quite unbecoming to a lady, could be heard a block away from the hospital.

LOY ANN BELL

SHORT STORY MYSTERIES

This story is fiction. I always wanted to go to the National Cutting Horse Futurity in Fort Worth, but I never made it, so I don't know how the barns there are laid out. However, with 500 to 600 of the nation's top three year olds competing every year, the show would definitely have adequate, organized stalls and facilities. So this setting is from my imagination.

Premeditated Revenge

    Elation gripped twenty-three-year-old Eddie Joe Slater as the announcer called his name at the National Cutting Horse Futurity in Fort Worth, Texas. Eddie hoped to win a good chunk of the $1,500,000 prize money, but he knew the competition would be rigorous. Horse owners from the U.S. and Europe employed expert trainers and entered their most talented three-year-old equine cutting stars.

    After working for a trainer named Doug Elliot from Odessa, Texas for five years, Eddie Joe had at last been allowed to compete instead of just exercising the horses. Of course, Doug had gotten first pick of the ones he thought were most likely to win, the "A" string, he called them. Eddie Joe had selected and trained a gray Quarter Horse gelding named "Little Blue" from the "B" string, and they had fit each other from the start.

Eddie's friends, a couple of exercise boys named Ted Larson and Afton Curtis, walked over to wish him luck. Ted wore a go-to-town light blue shirt with new Wranglers that enhanced his athletic, 5'11" frame, and with his blond handlebar mustache, he resembled a gunslinger from an old cowboy movie. On the other hand, Afton barely stood 5'7" and weighed 150 pounds. The wiry nineteen-year-old pulled a can of snuff from his hind pocket, pulled out a hefty pinch and crammed it into his mouth.

"You've been telling us how good that gray horse is, Idaho." Ted had dubbed the nickname on Eddie Joe because he hailed from the northern state. "Now show us how good he is."

Eddie set his jaw. "I'm sure gonna try."

Afton gave him a thumbs-up as the Idaho cowboy rode Blue through the pavilion gate. Inside, Doug Elliot, his boss, stood holding the reins to a horse he'd already shown. Doug nodded and Eddie figured it was his boss's way of telling him to loosen up and not let nerves spoil his performance.

Eddie jerked his mind back to the task at

SHORT STORY MYSTERIES

hand and sized up the milling herd of Hereford yearlings. He had two and a half minutes to show his horse's ability. Which calf should he cut? If he picked a lethargic one, it would move too slow and his horse wouldn't be able to display his athletic ability. If he picked one that was too fast, it could possibly slip past Little Blue, which would cost him points. Which one would work best so his mount's cow sense, athletic ability, intelligence, and speed could be exhibited?

The cowboy cued the gray horse to move toward the herd by leaning forward slightly and squeezing his legs. Blue calmly, methodically, moved the herd to the center of the arena, and let the cattle slowly flow past and drift into the corner. Ears cocked forward, poised with his weight balanced over his hindquarters, the gelding let the cattle trot by until only one remained.

The steer looked at Blue crouched in his path, then ran as hard as he could go, attempting to rejoin the herd. The battle began. Blue leaped in front of the calf, blocking him. The yearling changed directions, so the horse made a 180 degree turn and went with him. The calf made it fifteen feet before the horse outdistanced him. The young Hereford reversed, attempted to duck past, but again Little Blue barricaded him. Every time the steer tried to run by, Blue stood crouched in the way. Running from one side of the arena to the other, the calf kept ducking and turning until, unable to outmaneuver the horse, he finally stopped, "nailed down" near the center of the arena. With a frustrated expression on his face, the white-face turned his back to the gelding. Blue had won the battle. Eddie put his hand on the gray's neck in front of the saddle, signaling him to "quit" the calf.

The cowboy turned Blue around and headed back to the herd. With over a minute left, Eddie needed to work another calf ASAP. He'd already demonstrated how well the horse could quietly sort cattle, so this time he "peeled" a steer off the outer edge of the herd. Faster than the first one, this calf also ducked first one way, then the other. Head-to-head, horse and steer struggled in their dual, Little Blue always keeping the calf under control. The buzzer blew, but Eddie didn't signal the Quarter Horse to "quit" the steer until it turned away and stopped.

Eddie felt Doug's eyes on him as he rode out the gate. *Doug's gonna be proud of me,* he thought.

A few minutes later, the announcer's voice boomed, "Score for Number 384 is 76!" With a possible 80 points, 76 was an excellent score.

Eddie was ecstatic. That score would be

hard to beat. Friends rushed to congratulate him and Eddie knew what he'd always known—he *could* train a top cutting horse as well as any professional trainer. In the first three go-rounds, he'd done well; he was leading the average, the big money. Now all he had to do was to earn a good score in the one remaining round of competition to win a huge piece of the $1,500,000 prize money! It would be possible for him to be able to rent a barn/arena facility, buy some calves to work, or make a deal with a feed lot to use their cattle. People would bring their horses to him for training because at the biggest, most prestigious show in the nation, he'd proved he could train a top cutting horse. His record at the NCHA Futurity would establish the career he wanted to pursue for the rest of his life.

Ted and Afton hurried toward him as he rode out of the arena.

"Way to go, Idaho." Ted grinned and slapped Eddie on the leg while Afton gave him another thumbs-up.

Ted's boss, Bill Frey, sauntered over. Fifty-five years old and six foot three, Bill had a sloped forehead and a square jaw that depicted stubbornness. Frey had never uttered a word to Eddie before. "I don't like that jerk you work for, kid," he said, "but I gotta tell ya, you're a hell of a hand."

Eddie nearly fell off his horse at the compliment.

Troy Payton, the man Afton worked for, stopped en route to the arena when he overheard Bill's remarks. Troy was a thin man of medium height. His carrot-red hair showed beneath his silver belly hat and his green eyes twinkled as he said, "That's right, son. You've got three good go-rounds under your belt, so you stand a good chance of winning this shindig. Boy, would that burn some fannies around here!"

"You can come to work for me anytime, kid," Bill said. "If that jerk, Elliot, don't treat ya right, you just let me know."

"I second the offer." Troy smiled.

"Thanks," Eddie replied, but the Idaho cowboy didn't intend to take them up on their offers. He already had plans for his future. He excused himself by saying, "I'd better take care of Blue. He's certainly earned it."

Riding to the horse's stall, he unsaddled, rewarded Little Blue with a sliced-up apple, and "cooled" the gelding out by walking him for the next half an hour. He gave the gray an invigorating rubdown, absorbined his legs to keep the muscles limber. He didn't want Blue to have any "Charlie horse" kinks from the strenuous physical activity. Then he fed the gelding some good quality alfalfa/grass hay, a small ration of oats and gave him fresh water.

Ted and Afton walked up just as Eddie finished feeding. Both wore ear-to-ear grins.

"With all that money involved, I'll bet you were nervous," Afton said as he stuffed another chaw of tobacco in his mouth.

Eddie grinned back. "You better believe it! The butterflies are finally gone now. In fact, my belly thinks my throat's cut."

"There's a good Mexican restaurant down the street. Let's go get a bite to eat," Ted suggested. "You fed Doug's horses yet?"

"No, but Doug finished earlier and I cooled out all but one of his horses before I showed, and I've already taken care of that one, so I can feed anytime now."

Afton nodded. "We're all done. Come on, we'll help ya."

Feeding took less than five minutes with the three of them working. Afterward, they hopped in Ted's 2004 blue Ford pickup and went to chow down.

When they returned, Ted said, "Let's go play cards."

"Yeah, they've always got a good game going," Afton said.

"Where?" Eddie asked.

"The horse barns," Ted replied. "My boss keeps his hay in a vacant stall, but there's plenty of room for folding chairs. We tacked a piece of plywood over a barrel for a make-shift table. The only thing we can't do is smoke because of the fire danger."

"Naw, no drinking or staying up late for me. I'd better stay sharp," Eddie said, so they dropped him at the motel. A shower revitalized the young cowboy, but when he went to bed, exhilaration made sleep impossible. After tossing for an hour, he rose, donned his clothes and drove the two blocks to the barns.

Each long alleyway had five barns in it and each barn held ten horses; a space of 20 feet created a fire safety lane between the barns. An outdoor privy stood at each end of the alleyways.

Eddie located the "card room" in C alley in the third barn where Ted and Afton were playing for a nickel a point. He peeked in and watched Ted shuffle the cards. Ted looked up, spotted him, and nodded towards a chair. "Sit down, partner." He dealt Eddie in on the new hand. Eddie's cards ran lucky and soon a stack of nickels began to accumulate in front of him.

An hour later he needed to hit the restroom. "Do you go to the Sani-hut at the end of the alleyway?" he asked.

"Naw," Afton replied. "We go to the men's room by the office on A Alleyway. It's just as close and it's inside the building. It has a sink, even a shower. You can't miss it. There's a pay telephone sitting beside the door."

Eddie walked to A Alleyway, found the men's room, and made it back within five minutes.

Three hours and a huge pile of nickels later, Eddie Joe began to yawn.

He and Doug always checked on the horses just before going to bed, Doug at 10:00 and Eddie around 11:00 because he usually stayed up later than Doug. In F Alley where their horses were stalled, Eddie poked his head in the door and saw Blue standing in the darkness at the back of the stall. The gray walked over and nuzzled him.

"I'm proud of you, Blue," Eddie told him, stroking the glossy coat. "I knew you were a top horse and you've proved it. All we need is one more win, fella, and we'll take home a passel of money." He scratched behind the horse's ear; Blue leaned his head into the hand that alleviated the itchy spot. "Good night. See you in the morning," Eddie told the gelding.

When he returned to the motel, he had finally wound down enough so he could sleep.

As usual, he woke at 5:00 a.m. and fed the horses, then found Ted and Afton who had just finished feeding the horses entrusted to their care. A nearby McDonald's satisfied their craving for breakfast.

Before Doug competed on his A string horses, Eddie walked, trotted, and loped each one. His boss had only to mount and ride into the arena. Doug wore a frown, reflecting his frustration after he'd shown in the third go-round; his scores hadn't been high enough to place him in the money. Day money in the last go-round was the best he could hope for. Eddie knew their success depended on him and Blue.

Even on the days when Eddie didn't have to show, the young cowboy exercised Little Blue. Two days later, he was "up" in the fourth, the last go-round.

Eddie slipped the halter over Blue's head and led him out of the stall. Usually, the horse moved with confidence and trust in Eddie but not that time. His eyes had a wild look and he acted jittery, shying at his own shadow. In the bright sunlight, ugly red spur tracks showed on the gelding's shoulders. Alarm shot through Eddie. *Someone else has ridden Blue,* he thought.

SHORT STORY MYSTERIES

Apprehension and dread consuming him, he saddled and started to mount. Uncharacteristically, Blue jumped away, almost spilling the Idaho cowboy before he could hit the saddle. *Whoever rode this horse nearly scared him to death.* Hardly daring to move a foot, Eddie carefully rode Blue toward one of the exercise arenas.

He tried to warm the gray up slowly, but Blue's movements were jerky. The horse eyed every nook, cranny, other horses, and riders in the arena, leaping into the air and landing stiff-legged. Sweat began to pour off him. Eddie climbed off, unsaddled, and checked the saddle blanket for burrs. Nothing. He resaddled, then inspected the bit for sharp edges and checked the bridle to see if it fit properly. The equipment didn't look as though it had been tampered with. Eddie scratched his head. What had happened to Little Blue?

He tried riding the edge off the horse, to no avail. Eddie began to sweat, along with Blue. It would soon be time for the last go-round. The way the horse acted, Eddie Joe didn't think he'd even see a cow. In a panic, he walked the gelding until he heard the announcer say, "Eddie Joe Slater, in the hole." He was up next. He'd run out of time.

When the cowboy tried to ride the horse through the gate, Blue balked. One of the gatemen grabbed the horse's bridle and attempted to lead him into the arena. Blue nearly jumped on the man before they cleared the gate. Then the horse eyed a little boy holding a flag in his hand, and leaped four feet straight into the air. Eddie wondered if someone had substituted a dead ringer for Blue.

Their performance was terrible. Blue tried to run off. When Eddie got him stopped, the gelding stood quivering. Eddie Joe finally had to gig him with a spur to get him to take a step and the horse leaped forward. Instead of handling the cows quietly, Blue acted like an eggbeater in the herd and the cows scattered like a bunch of quail. If Eddie tried to rein him while he was moving, Blue lunged into the bit.

Acute embarrassment, then relief, settled over Eddie Joe when at last he escaped from the arena. He'd scored so well in his first three go-rounds, but his chance at the average, the high money, had just disintegrated. Along with his hopes for a cutting horse training career. He'd been convinced that Blue had what it took to become a champion, but doubts assailed him now.

Eddie had been suspicious when he saw the spur tracks on the gray's shoulders, but suddenly he thought he knew what had happened. Someone had ridden the gelding and badly abused him, "blowing" him to keep Eddie Joe from scoring high and taking home a lot of money. The cowboy's mind seemed like a jumbled snow screen, unable to focus, with thoughts flitting through it.

It had to be a jealous competitor who'd done this, but who? Eddie Joe was furious at his dreams being destroyed. He believed Blue would have worked right if he'd been left alone.

Ted and Afton trotted over to him.

"What happened?" Ted demanded.

Afton said, "I can't believe that's the same horse you've been showing."

Eddie just shook his head. He had no idea who could have committed such an atrocity, although a suspicion had begun to nag at him.

At 5:00 Ted and Afton insisted on taking Eddie to eat at a steakhouse to get his mind off the horrible performance. At first, they tried to cheer him up, but he didn't respond. He picked at his food, but didn't taste a bite.

When they pushed away from the table, he surprised Ted and Afton by saying, "Let's go play cards."

Ted glanced at him, surprised. "Now?"

Eddie shrugged. "Maybe it'll get my mind off what happened."

So they drove to the barn and played cards. No one moved from their seats until at 9:35, Ted made a trip to A Alley to use the restroom and, one by one, the rest of the guys took their turns. By 10:10 they were all back in their seats again playing their hands.

At 2:00 a.m., Eddie finally glanced at his watch. He felt as though his patutie had relocated up between his shoulder blades, he'd been sitting so long. "Gosh, we'd better hit the sack. Five o'clock is going to come pretty early. We aren't gonna get much sleep."

The others agreed and Ted, Afton, and Eddie Joe drove to the motel and went to bed. An hour or two passed before he finally drifted into a fitful sleep.

At 5:00 a.m. Ted called him. "We'd better get going, Eddie Joe."

The cowboy rolled out of bed and dressed.

They drove through the darkness to the barn. The lights spaced along the alleyway cast a dim light into the stalls. Eddie could barely see as he began placing blocks of alfalfa hay in the hanging feeders. He'd worked most of the way down F Alley when he started to take some hay into the next stall and spied a boot on the straw-covered floor! Dropping the hay, he opened the door and rushed in. Doug Elliot lay sprawled with his head cocked at an awkward angle. Blood oozing from Doug's head had flowed onto the amber-colored straw, staining it. Eddie froze, stared open mouthed for several moments before he could react.

"Help! Help!" he finally yelled. His shouting attracted Ted and a crowd of other early risers. Ted ran up and looked over the stall door.

"My God," he exclaimed. "Doug isn't moving. Somebody go call the cops!"

A cowboy yanked out his cell phone, trotted a few feet away, and dialed 911.

Sirens screaming, the police arrived in two cruisers. One of the uniformed cops asked where the body was located. Ted led the cop to the stall. After feeling for a carotid pulse and finding none, the cop ran to his car and radioed for homicide. He asked Eddie Joe to move the horse to another stall, then he began stringing yellow crime scene tape.

Within 20 minutes, a six foot, heavy-set detective with closely-cropped gray hair pulled up in an unmarked Chevy. He wore a navy pin-striped suit and his shiny black oxfords were covered with a coat of dust the moment he stepped out of the car. While inspecting the crime scene, he discovered a bloody baseball bat propped up against the inside of the stall, and poked his head out the door.

"Who found the body?" he asked.

"I did." Eddie Joe stepped forward.

"I'm Detective Simpson," the cop said.

"Did you know the deceased?"

"Yes. He was my boss."

After that Eddie lost track of time. Detective Simpson and his partner commandeered the barn office and began questioning everyone. Eddie told them how he always fed and exercised the horses and Doug had rewarded him by letting him show in the competition. "I owe Doug a great deal," he added.

"Have you any idea who might have wanted to kill him?"

Eddie thought about Bill Frey and Troy Payton. They'd both called Doug a jerk, but would they have killed him? Maybe yes, maybe no. Neither one had liked him. Eddie hesitated, then said, "No." How could he sic the cops on either of his supporters?

Simpson sent him a look that said he didn't totally believe the cowboy.

"And where were you last night from 10:00 p.m. until 2:00 a.m.?"

"We ate at Kirby's Steak House, then played cards from 7:00 until 2:00. Ted Larson, Afton Curtis and two other guys were with me."

Simpson nodded and wrote in his small notebook.

Ted, Afton, and Eddie were able to alibi one another as to their whereabouts the night before.

SHORT STORY MYSTERIES

When they met later, they agreed that Bill Frey might have committed the murder, but none of them had told the cops their suspicions because they liked Bill. But Bill and his wife came up with a strong alibi: they'd partied until the wee hours with relatives who lived in Ft. Worth.

The cops also considered Troy Payton but Troy had stayed at an uptown hotel, hadn't been able to sleep, and spent from 9:00 p.m. to 1:00 a.m. in the bar so he couldn't have done the deed either.

Doug's brother, Garth Elliot, arrived from Houston the next day to make the funeral arrangements. "I feel bad about Doug," he told Eddie, shaking his head. "We were never close, didn't see eye to eye, even when we were kids."

For three days, the police examined suspects, interviewing, and eliminating them. Several people had grudges against Doug, but they all had alibis. The police were at an impasse.

Garth Elliot asked if Eddie would trailer the horses back to Doug's place in El Paso and Eddie said he would. Garth started to walk off, then stopped abruptly and swung around. "Eddie, would you be interested in buying Doug's training facility?"

Eddie Joe's heart hit rock bottom. "I wish I could, but I don't have that kind of money."

"Not a problem," Garth said. "You can make payments. That is, if you're interested."

"You better believe I'm interested!" Eddie exclaimed.

"Good," Garth said. "We'll get together after everything's been probated and talk terms. Since I live clear down in the other end of the state, I don't want to have to worry about things up here. I've got problems enough running my own business." He headed for his red Cadillac. "I'll call you," he said over his shoulder.

With his mind in a fog, Eddie began loading the cutting horses. First thing he'd do was restart Little Blue, bring the horse along easy, and hopefully recondition him.

Ted walked up just as the Idaho cowboy finished tying the third horse in Doug's huge trailer. "Headed for Doug's place?" he asked.

"Yes. Detective Simpson said I could take the horses home."

Ted looked around to make sure no one was close enough to overhear their conversation. "Simpson told me they don't have a clue as to who killed Doug," he said carefully. "But I think I know who killed him."

"Who?" Eddie Joe demanded.

"You did," Ted replied.

"Me? Are you crazy?" Shock made Eddie's

eyes widen.

"Doug had a jealous streak. You took a reject horse from the B string and beat him on his A string horses," Ted said. "He couldn't stand that. So during the night, he took Little Blue out and jerked and spurred until he blew the horse's mind."

Eddie eyed Ted like a calf looking at a new gate.

Ted continued. "He did his best to destroy your chances of becoming a cutting horse trainer. You left to go to the men's room for a few minutes the night of the murder, but I don't think you went down to the restroom at A Alley. Instead, you went to F Alley where Doug's horses are stalled 'cause you knew he always checked the horses at 10:00."

"That's quite a theory." Eddie said.

"You had a baseball bat stashed in the stall to use on Doug. You would have wiped your prints off after you killed him." He reached up and twirled his blond mustache. "Apparently I'm the only one who noticed that you left at exactly 9:58 p.m. and were gone at least ten minutes."

Eddie thought for a moment, then asked, "What do you intend to do?"

"Absolutely nothing. Doug was a miserable human being." Ted grinned. "That man needed killing. I'd have helped if you'd only asked."

LOY ANN BELL

SHORT STORY MYSTERIES

THE FIGHT

On a muggy Friday night in June, 1928, Mat Kelso fogged his black Model T pickup up the hard-packed dirt road towards Gilmore, Idaho. From half a mile away, the twenty-six-year-old could see the Corner Bar among the many tents and shacks which had been "thrown up" virtually overnight when silver and lead were discovered in the surrounding mountains. With its wooden construction, dark brown paint, and a three-holer outhouse, the bar stood out like a rose in a briar patch. Cars, pickups, and even some trucks, filled the rutted vacant lot beside it, so Mat had to park half a block away and walk back.

The noise level slapped him in the face

when he opened the door. Men stood two deep at the bar, laughing and talking, while a gray, smoky haze drifted toward the ceiling. He glanced at the poker table in the corner, noting that only one chair remained open. He'd have to hurry. He waved at Chuck, the grizzled, gray haired owner/bartender, who grabbed a glass and shoved it under the keg spigot. By the time Mat elbowed his way through the smelly, just-off-shift miners, truck drivers, ranchers, cowboys, and ranch hands in dirty shirts and tattered, dusty Levis, Chuck had his beer waiting on the bar.

"Boy, this place is jumpin' tonight." Mat fished a fifty-cent piece from his pocket, plopped it down, took a swig of brew, and wiped his mouth with the back of his hand.

"Just the way we like it," Chuck said, scooping up the coin. He made change and slapped it on the bar. "See ya later." He scurried away to wait on another customer.

Mat cowboyed at the Bar J Ranch and always headed for town on weekends. Standing five-ten, he always tried to keep his face shaved and his hair cut. A nice girl named Mary Adkins liked him, he knew, but he hadn't gotten around to asking her to marry him; if she said "yes", it might scare him out of twenty years of life. He liked to drink and get wild, but most of all, he loved to play cards

SHORT STORY MYSTERIES

and it was a sure bet that a wife wouldn't appreciate that. In fact, his girlfriend had already voiced her disapproval.

He headed for the poker table and grabbed the vacant seat. His buddy, Dan Vicerine, glanced up and nodded as Mat sat down. Dan must have had a good hand, because when he held good cards, his tattle-tale m.o. was to be quiet, not laughing or joking as usual. And right then he was completely engrossed in his cards, gripping them with white-knuckled hands. He took his card playing seriously.

Most of the players were miners, hard cases that Mat played poker with every weekend. "Poncho" Avery was named for his enormous pot belly; Joe Morales was a half-breed Mexican, quick to go for a knife when riled; Curly Gillis had evidently been given the nickname when he'd had hair; and Bull Parker was a big, brown haired giant with a full beard that covered the lower half of his face. After combing the hills or digging under the ground all day, they were a grubby looking bunch of scalawags who seldom bothered to clean up before they came to town. If Mat hadn't had the card-playing bug so badly, he wouldn't have associated with the rank-smelling rascals. And they were a dangerous bunch---quick to anger and quicker to fight.

One newcomer introduced himself as "John" and played cards with them at the gambling table that Friday night. Mat pegged him as a rancher because the tall man wore an old straw hat, a plaid pearl-snapped western shirt, and scuffed boots and spurs. Dirt and dust covered his clothes, but his hair was nicely trimmed and he looked as though he at least took a bath on Saturday nights. Fitting right in, John cracked jokes and matched drinks with the rest of them.

After five hours of sitting, betting, and drawing cards, only getting up when they had to hit the outhouse, they were all quite drunk. Even the five spectators watching the game were looped, hanging onto the backs of chairs for balance.

Mat looked across the table. Poncho had begun to scowl. *Oh, no,* Mat thought. *When Poncho gets that expression, it isn't long before he picks a fight with somebody.*

As if on cue, Poncho left the cards face down that he'd just been dealt, looked around, and said in a loud voice, "I found silver today. Any of you SOBs think you're tough enough to steal my claim, I'll kill ya!" He searched for a candidate to vent his desire to clobber someone.

The other players became totally engrossed in their cards and ignored him. His scowl deepened. Glaring, he tried to catch someone's eye, but no one would look at him. Disappointed at not finding any takers, he finally picked up his cards and the tension evaporated for the moment.

Five minutes later, Mat's buddy, Dan, said, "Hey, Mat, are ya ridin' many colts now?"

"Naw," Mat replied. "The boss has me fixin' fence. I hate that job somethin' fierce."

"Don't blame ya," Dan replied.

Scrutinizing his cards, Mat scratched his head.

Poncho said, "Awww, neither one of ya've ever done a day's work in yur lives."

"You ain't never worked on a ranch, have ya?" Mat said dryly.

"Don't need to. I can look at you two and tell yur a couple a wusses."

Dan started to stand up. Mat grabbed his belt and pulled him back down in his chair. "He's just drunk," Mat whispered. "So're you. For that matter, I guess I am too."

"That's no excuse for him runnin' off at the mouth," Dan growled.

"Forget it." Mat studied his cards. A couple of minutes later, Dan finally picked up his hand. Mat didn't think his buddy could even see the cards. Actually, Mat couldn't see his cards very well either. They kept going out of focus. He stared at them, decided he had a lousy hand. He wondered how much, if anything, he should bet on it.

The game continued.

Less than ten minutes later, Joe Moreles jumped up, glared at Bull Parker across the table. "You dealin' offa da bottom," he accused, and from nowhere, his switchblade appeared.

Bull Parker leaped to his feet also, nearly knocking the table over, causing cards and money to spill everywhere. "You got no business callin' me a cheat, you damned greaser," he roared.

The little Mexican didn't waste any time. He sprang at Parker, sliced at Bull's huge, hairy, muscled arm. Stunned, Bull watched the bright red blood spewing, let out a beller, and lunged at Morales. The Mexican side-stepped, gave the big man a solid jab in the nose as Parker's momentum carried him past. Blood gushed from Bull's nose too.

Dan hopped up and exclaimed, "I knew he was dealing off the bottom of the deck!"

"No, he weren't." Curly Gillis stood up also, a belligerent look on his face. "I'd a knowed it if he hadda been."

Dan hit him square in the mouth.

From then on, they all agreed to disagree. Within 30 seconds, everybody in the place was swinging at somebody. A table spectator charged at

Mat who instinctively hit the guy over the head with a beer glass. It shattered, cutting Mat's hand. Then someone blindsided Mat and he found himself crawling, his hand leaving bloody palm prints on the floor. He hoped no one would step or fall on him. Twice he tried to regain his feet but both times someone hit him before he could straighten up.

Naturally a bartender couldn't abstain while everybody else drank heartily, so Chuck had been drinking with his customers. As a result, he was plastered too. He attempted to leap over the bar to settle the fight but fell back among the bottles on the wall, scattering them and breaking several. He stood upright, trotted around the end of the bar instead, and joined the unadulterated brawl.

They were having a roarin' good time, really tearing up the joint when the shooting began. Afterward, nobody seemed to know who'd started the firing, but suddenly bullets started whizzing everywhere. Already on the floor, Mat crawled behind the poker table that was rolling around. Knowing it had been specially constructed of plywood and mahogany, he wondered how it had gotten tipped over. He peeked out. Dan stood against the wall waving his Colt 45, yelling, "Come and get me, ya sons a bitches! I'll give ya a taste of lead. You won't have to dig for it anymore." He aimed the Colt at the crowded bar and shot. Whether from getting hit with a fist or from being shot, an old miner slowly sank to the floor.

Matt was horrified. Somebody's going to get hurt. Or killed.

Then he spied Bull Parker waving a .32 pistol, yelling and shooting too. Mat decided if he made it out of this fracas, he'd be a lover, not a fighter, from then on. He might even give up cards. But right now, he had to disarm Dan before his friend killed somebody. However, Bull was standing by the door and Mat found himself pinned in a cross fire. Whichever way he turned, he would be exposed to one of the shooters.

He took his chances on Dan because, even drunk, he didn't *think* his buddy would shoot him. Also he didn't want Dan to spend the rest of his life in prison for killing someone. Mat started rolling the poker table toward his friend, crawling behind it. Two bullets just missed him as they pierced the wood, leaving jagged holes. Splinters rained down. He dropped to his belly and slithered across the floor like a snake. Finally, he got close enough to reach out, grab Dan's ankle, and give it a yank. Dan came crashing down, cussing.

"Shut up, you fool," Mat hissed in his ear. "I may have just saved your life." He pulled Dan behind the table, anchoring him to the floor.

SHORT STORY MYSTERIES

Flailing his arms and legs, Dan nearly escaped but Mat hung on, pinned him as if he were a bug—and wrestled the gun away so he couldn't fire it anymore.

Fifteen minutes passed before everybody quit throwing punches and the shooting stopped. Chuck looked around with disgust. The joint was trashed. Chuck evidently didn't realize that he'd helped trash it.

"You bastards is gonna pay damages or you're outta here!" he declared, knowing he had them over a barrel. None of them wanted to be banished from their favorite playpen.

Suddenly, an old cowboy at the end of the bar said, "Somebody's been shot!"

"Let me see." Chuck clawed his way to where the cowboy stood staring at the floor.

Sure enough, a body lay sprawled beside the bar, blood soaking through a blue denim work shirt.

Chuck checked for a pulse. The miner wasn't breathing. "Just look at what you guys 'uv done," he exclaimed.

Then someone discovered another body lying by the back wall where the poker table usually sat. "Hey, there's two of 'em!"

Mat recognized the second body as "John", the rancher who'd played cards all night. Mat's eyes protruded and he felt like a huge hand was squeezing his heart. *Oh magosh, Dan may have shot him!*

"The deputy'll come down from Leadore and git us," someone said, the voice radiating fear.

"Let's bury 'em," somebody else urged.

"Well, we don't know who shot 'em," Chuck said reasonably, the liquor causing his words to slur. "Let's get rid of the bodies. Then nobody can pin this on us."

"Where we gonna bury 'em? The ground around here's as hard as a rock," an old miner pointed out.

"It rained night before last. There's some soft ground on ole man Osgood's place," someone else suggested. "We can bury 'em there."

Chuck began issuing orders.

Four tipsy volunteers silently trudged out the door to dig the graves. Mat heard a couple of engines fire up, bounce out of the parking lot, and head down the graveled Main Street. With Dan staggering behind carrying the victims' hats, Mat, Chuck, Bull, and Curly hauled the bodies out and put them in the back of Chuck's pickup.

Mat and Chuck walked back into the bar where Chuck announced, "You guys keep yur durned mouths shut about this. Nobody knows nuthin', got it? Now go home. Party's over for tonight." He waited until his customers meekly filed out, pulled the door shut behind them, and locked it.

Mat and Dan climbed in the cab with Chuck while Bull and Curly squeezed onto the narrow tailgate. When they reached Osgood's place, they spotted the shadowy gravediggers in the headlights. Mounds of fresh soil were piled beside two gaping holes. Chuck backed up the pickup. They slid the bodies into the shallow graves and covered them. Due to the seriousness of the situation, all the partiers had begun to sober up. Mat began to worry that the law would hear about the fiasco. Too many people were involved to keep it quiet and too many of them liked to talk.

But evidently everyone kept the silence because no repercussions came from the law. Two weeks passed and Mat had begun to think they'd gotten away with it.

Then one day, as Mat waited in line at the mercantile store to purchase a couple of work shirts, an elderly woman walked in the door. She wore glasses and her hair was tucked into a bun at the back of her neck. "My husband's disappeared," she said to the store keeper, her voice cracking. "He had to go to Mackay on Friday two weeks ago and he never came home. I think something's happened to him." Tears spilled down her cheeks. She removed her glasses and dabbed at the tears with a clean white handkerchief.

Mat froze. "Have you got a picture of him?"

She pulled a worn photo from her purse and held it out with a shaking hand.

The man named John who'd played poker that fateful Friday night smiled at him from the photograph. Mat's face turned ghostly white.

The woman stopped crying and studied his expression. "You've seen him, haven't you?

Mat said, "Maybe." Ever since that night, he'd felt guilty. He liked the woman's neat appearance and her manner; she reminded him of his mother. He knew it would help her deal with the death if she could just have closure.

"Wait here. I'll be back." He trotted over to the Corner Bar.

"We gotta problem." He told Chuck about the matronly woman.

"I gotta see that picture," Chuck said as he shucked his soiled apron. "I can't believe we buried that guy that night. We shoulda called the deputy. If we hadn't all been so drunk, we woulda." After asking one of his customers to watch the bar for a few minutes, he and Mat headed for the mercantile store.

Chuck's face turned pale as he stared at the

SHORT STORY MYSTERIES

photo. He glanced at Mat and gave an almost imperceptible nod. "We'll be back," he told the woman. We've got to check out something." Apprehensive, the two walked back across the street.

Two of the men who'd dug the graves two weeks before were drinking beer at the bar.

"Come on," Chuck told them. "Grab your shovels."

"Oh oh," one of them muttered.

"What're we gonna do?" the other asked.

"We gotta dig up those fellas we buried a couple weeks ago." Chuck headed for the door with Mat right behind him. The two customers climbed down off their stools and followed.

They all piled in Chuck's pickup and drove to the burial site. The soil hadn't had time to pack, so it didn't take them long to uncover the bodies. Brown blood had caked on the shirtfront of the miner who'd stood by the bar.

"Yup, that's the old geezer," Chuck said. "See, he's been shot in the chest." The bullet hole showed plainly.

"Let's see where John got hit," Mat said, dreading to look.

They examined John's body closely but neither of them could see where a bullet had entered the front of the body.

"I don't see anything," Mat said, perplexed. "Let's check the other side."

Chuck and one of the grave diggers grabbed the body, turned it over and studied it to see where the bullet or bullets had penetrated the man's back. Nothing. No sign of an injury.

"Good God," Chuck breathed. "There's no holes in 'im!"

He and Mat stared at one another, their faces turning an ashen gray as the realization hit. The man, John, hadn't been shot. He'd only been drunk, passed out and they'd buried him alive. He'd suffocated.

SHORT STORY MYSTERIES

Through the years, several of my friends raced their horses under flat saddle on the track or hitched them to chariots. This fictional story is based on my knowledge of the racing game.

EASY LOVIN'

Black mane and tail streaming, Easy Lovin' thundered down the Jerome, Idaho race track. The little jockey perched on the black Quarter Horse's back like a burr, the two blending together as they crossed the finish line.

My friend, Glen Westmore, and I punched our stopwatches. I glanced at my watch, then stared at it, unable to believe my eyes. Twenty-two seconds flat for 220 yards and the two-year-old wasn't even running at top speed. "Wow! That colt's a movin' machine," I exclaimed.

A lopsided grin transformed Glen's dark-complexioned face. He tipped his old black Stetson back, exposing the sweat ring on his black hair. "Told ja that colt could fly." Taking four quick steps, his five-ten-body rose in the air, and his heels clicked together with a pop.

His wife, Debbie, watched him and shook her head, swishing her blonde ponytail that protruded from the back of her Boise State baseball cap, which she always referred to as her "football cap." Nearly as tall as Glen, she resembled a big, beautiful doll. "Now, Glen, don't be countin' your chickens before…"

"I know, I know, before they're hatched." Glen interrupted. "But I'm right about this one." He put his arm around her and gave her a quick hug. "Honey, we're gonna make a lotta money with Easy Lovin.'"

His best friend, Dutch Hogue, cigarette dangling from the side of his mouth, grabbed my wrist, peeked at the watch and laughed gleefully. "Summer racing circuit, here we come!" He attempted a heel-click too, but didn't quite get his six-foot-two frame high enough and nearly landed on his patutie. His cigarette fell, his straw cowboy hat floated to the ground, and his light brown hair spilled into his face, but his hazel eyes were gleaming.

The racing bug has struck my friends I thought.

Impatiently, we waited for the jockey to bring the prancing colt back. Adrenaline-fired, the shiny onyx colt shook his head, wanting to run.

"Good job," Glen told the little jockey. He held the horse while the small man dismounted, then took off the bridle and the pancake saddle and slid a halter over the colt's head.

Lighting another cigarette as he walked to the horse trailer, Dutch untied his chestnut "pony" horse, and swung up. "I'll cool out the speedster," he said. Grabbing the lead rope, he urged the chestnut into a walk, the colt dancing alongside.

"I have never owned a horse that could run like this one," Glen said.

"He's built well too," I commented. "And with that glistening black color, he's gorgeous."

Glen's eyes glowed. "I raised him from a baby. If he runs like I think he's going to, we'll make a fortune in stud fees after we retire him. We'll be rich, Deb."

Debbie didn't say anything.

"We oughta celebrate," Glen continued.

"Don't forget. Clarence Taber's birthday party is tonight," I reminded him.

An old race horse trainer, Clarence had reached eighty three years of age and for six months, his family had been planning a barbeque/party. The old man had successfully raced many Quarter Horses, usually wore a smile, and constantly spouted Mark Twain-type witty remarks. Everyone loved him.

"Oh magosh, I'd forgotten," Glen admitted. He thought a moment and perked up. "Hey, we'll celebrate Clarence's birthday and Easy Lovin's future at the same time. We'll be there, right honey?" He glanced at Debbie for affirmation. She nodded.

"It's at seven thirty. I'll see you then." I crawled in my pickup and drove home, feeling Glen's exhilaration as if Easy Lovin' were mine.

At Clarence's party, Glen couldn't keep from bragging. "You know that black colt I named Easy Lovin'?" He searched the old trainer's face. "He can really run."

Clarence liked to tease. "So can I," he said. "But not very far and not very fast."

Glen refused to take the bait. "I'm telling' ya, this is a once-in-a-lifetime horse," he said stubbornly.

Clarence grinned. "What kind of time's he runnin'?"

Glen told him what the colt had clocked that morning.

"That is impressive." Clarence agreed. "Go easy with him and keep him sound."

"I will," Glen promised. "By the way, I named him "Easy Lovin'" since he's by Easy Jet."

"You shouldn't be braggin' on the colt, Glen," Debbie told him. "It's bad luck."

I noticed she hustled Glen and Dutch out the door as quickly as she could without appearing rude.

Personally, I thought she was right. Better not to say anything. Jealousy did funny things to people sometimes, especially around the race tracks where huge amounts of money were bet. Equine stars had had eyes put out or killed in other ways. Besides, Glen could talk all he wanted, but the colt would either run fast at the actual races or he wouldn't.

After they left, I yakked with Clarence and his family for another hour before heading home at 10:30. Tired from hauling hay for my horses that morning, I hit the sack.

At 6:00 a.m. I rose as usual, dressed, and trotted out to feed. Two yearling colts, a bay and a buckskin, nickered at me. They were my hopes for the track the next year and Glen had offered to help me train them. I could hardly wait to see if they had any speed. Guess the racing bug had struck me too.

Thirty minutes later, I was frying bacon and a couple of eggs for breakfast when my cell phone rang. Very seldom anyone called before 7:00 so I quickly grabbed it and answered. A piercing, high-pitched cacophony assailed my eardrum.

"There's been an accident," Eric Stanton, a sheriff's deputy friend of mine, blurted. "Glen Westmore's been killed."

Shock hit me; I felt numb. "Glen? Gosh, I just saw him last night. What on earth happened?"

"He was run over by his four-horse trailer."

"At his house?"

"Yep."

"That must have been awful for Debbie."

"That's the main reason I called," Eric said. "She's in hysterics. Could you please come over and take her to the hospital emergency room? I'm the first one on the scene and nobody else is here yet."

That explained the strange noise in the background. "I'll be right there," I replied. "Did you call Dutch?"

"Yes, he's on his way. I'll need to talk to you two and get your statements. You were among the last people to see him alive. But let's get Debbie taken care of first."

"See ya in a few minutes." I hung up, turned the stove burners off, and ran for my pickup.

When I pulled into Glen and Debbie's driveway, the Sheriff and two deputies were in the barnyard hovering around Glen's pickup and horse trailer. Another deputy was stringing yellow crime scene tape.

I'd stumbled halfway up the walk when Debbie came tearing out of the house and flung herself at me. Strands of stringy blonde hair hung down into her pasty white face. Her eyes were red, her cheeks tear-streaked. She grabbed me around the neck in a choke hold.

"Oh, what am I going to do?" she sobbed. "I can't live without Glen."

Eric walked out behind her. Dutch trudged along behind, his face an ashen gray.

Looking pointedly at Eric, I said, "Let's get you to the hospital, Debbie. Help me, Dutch."

I untangled her arms from my neck, and slipped my arm around her. She leaned against me as we walked to the pickup. Dutch ground his cigarette out with his boot and opened the door for her. Together we managed to help her get in. She kept moaning softly and I wouldn't have been surprised if she'd passed out on the spot. Dutch climbed in and sat on the passenger side.

Eric said, "I'll meet you at the court house. Call me when you get through at the hospital, okay?" He mouthed "thanks" to me and headed for the barnyard to assist the other lawmen.

The emergency room doctor gave Debbie a shot of Demerol and ordered her to stay, at least for 24 hours. I gave the admittance clerk all the information I could and she retrieved an insurance policy number from a recent file when Glen had had his tonsils removed.

As we walked out the hospital door, I called Eric.

"I'll meet you in ten minutes," he promised.

Dutch and I grabbed a cup of coffee to go at Choate's Drive In. "So what happened?" I asked, knowing he'd probably been there when the accident occurred.

He gulped a swig of coffee and nearly dropped the cup as the steaming liquid burned his throat. "I dunno. Glen said he was going in the house, told me to park the trailer next to the horse barn where he always kept it. I started to pull around so I could back it in." He shook his head, took another drink, and swallowed it as he recalled the moment. He set the coffee on the dashboard.

"So what happened, Dutch?" I persisted.

He stared into space. "I felt a bump," he said slowly. "The trailer ran over something. I stopped, but when I started to slip the gearshift into park, I accidentally hit reverse instead and backed up."

"And ran over the bump again," I supplied,

knowing, but dreading to hear what the "bump" had been.

"Yeah." He covered his face with his hands and began to cry, his shoulders shaking. "My best friend and I ran over him," he blubbered.

I reached over and patted him on the back, attempting to console him. When he'd regained some semblance of control, I drove us to the orange-colored brick court house. The deputy's car was already there when we pulled into the parking area.

"Let me talk to Dutch first." Eric headed down the hall to his office and Dutch followed

Nearly an hour passed before they reappeared. Dutch looked drained. He plopped down in the chair next to me like a sack of potatoes, blinked several times, and began rubbing his temples.

"Your turn," Eric said to me.

I related yesterday's events, but couldn't tell him anything about the accident. How could I? I wasn't there. In answer to his question, I told him I hadn't noticed anything different in Glen's or Dutch's attitudes toward one another. Eric said a Coroner's Inquest would be held.

"Why?" I demanded. "It was an accident."

"Yes, but it's standard procedure in a case

like this." Eric rubbed his eye. "Hey, I don't make any determinations. The Coroner, the Sheriff, and the Prosecuting Attorney evaluate the evidence and rule accordingly."

"It probably scared Dutch to death when he hit the first bump," I rationalized. "He didn't have any idea how many feet he traveled before he got the pickup in park."

"Maybe," Eric said noncommittally. "They'll decide at the inquest."

"I've run around with Glen and Dutch a lot and I can tell you they were the best of friends, played pranks on one another and everybody else and had a lot of fun together."

"I know," he replied. "I've seen them too."

* * *

Debbie looked pretty rough when we picked her up at St. Benedict's Hospital the next morning, but at least she wasn't crying.

Four days later, people filled the mortuary to attend the funeral because Glen had been well liked. Debbie's sister, Crystal, came from Colorado and stayed with her a week, helping her recuperate from the shock. I offered to feed the horses, but Debbie said Dutch had already offered to take care of the chores.

When I dropped by a couple of days after

the funeral, Debbie said she'd made arrangements with Dutch to keep Easy Lovin' in race training. "Glen would have wanted the colt to have his chance at greatness," she said.

That's for sure, I thought.

The Coroner's Inquest ruled Glen's death to be accidental. When the Sheriff announced the determination, Dutch quit puffing on his cigarette and exhaled a deep breath that sounded like air escaping from a balloon.

During that summer, Debbie paid the entry fees for the colt and Dutch trained him slowly and methodically, never letting him get excited in the starting gate. Easy Lovin's feet were carefully trimmed and shod by the best farrier in Magic Valley. The glistening black colt seemed to float down the track when the jockey breezed him, and as Dutch directed, the jockey never asked the youngster for top speed.

At his first race, another horse bumped Easy Lovin' as he broke from the starting gate causing him to run second, but he won his next five races handily. Dutch always invited me to go along when he hauled the ebony colt to the tracks. After all, I had a personal interest in the horse since I'd thought so much of Glen. Every time Easy ran, I screamed and yelled until my voice nearly quit, helping him across the finish line.

The race meet at Pocatello came up midway through the summer season. Debbie rode with us this time, and listened to our continuous race banter about Easy Lovin' and the horses he'd be running against. I knew she had to be delighted at Easy Lovin's record to date.

The first night of the meet, I was visiting with some of the guys at the horse barn when I suddenly realized I'd left my cell phone in the pickup. Because I was expecting an important call, I hiked over to the parking lot to retrieve my phone. I smelled cigarette smoke and heard familiar voices, which caused me to pause for a moment in the darkness to listen. Debbie's and Dutch's voices came across plainly, their words distinct in the night air.

"You said you loved me," Debbie said, "but when it came right down to it, you couldn't do it."

Do what? I wondered.

"No, I couldn't do it," Dutch retorted. "But you jumped in that truck and never hesitated. How many times did you run over him before you thought he was dead? Even drug him, for hell's sake." Disgust emanated from his voice.

"I did it for us," Debbie whispered hoarsely. "So we could be together."

"Well, you got away with it, but I'm

thinking' you might just do the same to me some day."

A loud pop reverberated across the parking area.

"Don't ever hit me again, you bloodthirsty bitch," Dutch said venomously.

Debbie began to cry. "You never loved me," she accused. "All you really wanted was that bloomin' horse."

"I did want the black," he admitted. "But the price was too high. Now, every time I look at you, I get sick to my stomach."

I heard his footsteps stomp off.

Good grief! I thought. *They planned Glen's murder together, but Dutch couldn't go through with it. So Debbie killed Glen. And I didn't have a clue. If I go to the police now, it will be my word against hers. She's committed the perfect murder, but she's lost the person she loved so much—-Dutch.*

Hmmmm... So much for easy lovin', I thought.

LOY ANN BELL

SHORT STORY MYSTERIES

My friend, Bobby Jones, played music at a guest ranch in Arizona for several years and the ranch owners first thought this episode occurred on their land. Intrigued, Bobby asked me to research and record this factual happening about the stage coach, driver and three passengers. The story, Johnny Jump-Up, won 1st place in the Creative Nonfiction Category of the Idaho Writers' League 2011 Contest.

Johnny Jump-Up

One hot afternoon in June, 1880, six lathered bay horses pulled the marred, weathered stagecoach up the steep mountain road into Mineral Park, Arizona. The stage driver, a tall, slender man named "Johnny Jump-Up" Upshaw hauled back on the reins, and hollered "Whoa!" A swirling cloud of dust engulfed the coach as it stopped in the thriving mining town.

The foreman of the Cerbat Mining Company, William L. Thiebert, stepped out of the mine office. He was a robust man with a dark brown handlebar mustache. "We got a big shipment for ya tonight, Johnny," he said.

A score of mines operated in the Cerbat Mountains and, since the 1870's, they often shipped gold, large sums of money and other valuables on the stages.

Johnny glanced around but didn't see any riders waiting. "You hired some guys to ride shotgun, didn't you?"

"Naw, we haven't had any robberies lately out in that god-forsaken country," the foreman replied.

"That's true," Johnny agreed. "Just the same, I'd feel better if I had some protection while I'm hauling such a big shipment."

"Aw, you'll be all right." Thiebert pursed his lips.

Yeah, maybe nobody will hold me up, Johnny thought, *but if they do, it's my life that's on the line, not yours.*

Against his better judgment, he finally succumbed to the foreman's persuasion and agreed to haul the shipment.

Thiebert headed into the building. "Come on boys, let's get this loaded."

With a great deal of effort, six men lugged a large wooden strong box reinforced with iron out to the stage and wedged it under the front seat. The box held $100,000 from the Cerbat Mining Company and $10,000 to $20,000 apiece from several smaller mining companies, bringing the total to over $200,000, mostly in gold ingots.

"I've got three passengers too. This is an awful heavy load!" Johnny exclaimed. "Good thing I'm going to be changing horses at Beale Springs. These're 'bout to give out."

He climbed aboard, jumped up and cracked his whip over the six horses to get them started, then yelled, "Let's go, ya cayouses." The horses leaned into the traces and slowly the stage began to move. At the street's end, Johnny turned around and headed back through town and on down the road, destination—Needles, California.

That evening he pulled into Beale Springs (about two miles northwest of present-day Kingman.) The passengers disembarked, tired and dusty. While the men from the station harnessed and hitched the fresh horses, Johnny and the passengers made their trips to the outhouse. Then they all sat down at the large table inside the stage stop and gratefully ate a bowl of hot stew, washing it down with a cool drink of water from the nearby natural springs.

Stars had begun to sparkle in the night sky when the passengers climbed back into the stage.

Accustomed to making runs during the nights when it was cooler, Johnny clambered up on the driver's seat, stood up and cracked his whip over the teams.

The old stage road ran southeast between the Black and Cerbat Mountain ranges, then turned southwest. Jagged mountains, craggy canyons, deep ravines, high mesas, flash-flood washes, and deadly fissures made the country extremely dangerous. The stage coach would ferry across the Colorado River at Whipple's' Crossing south of Needles and continue on into California.

At ten p.m., four men helped change the teams at the next stage stop which was located seventeen miles south in the Sacramento Valley of western Arizona. The stage pulled out on schedule. It made good time as it rolled through the night, but just as Johnny rounded a rocky bend, three men suddenly rode out of a sandy wash with their guns drawn.

"Hold it!" a black haired man with a droopy mustache yelled. Dust covered his shabby black hat and he rode a mangy sorrel horse. The driver recognized him—"Hualapai Joe" Desredo—and stopped the horses. Johnny knew the splay-footed, mean, annoying little cuss rumored to be half Hualapai Indian would have no qualms about killing him and his passengers.

"Everybody out of the stage!" Joe ordered.

"And throw down your guns."

The passengers reluctantly climbed out. The two men, a local doctor and a minister, began babbling, "Don't shoot! We'll give you everything we have."

One of the outlaws, Lefty Barnes, stood five foot five inches, a little, dried-up excuse of a man. "I'll see if the gold's in the coach," he said, getting off his horse. He discovered the wooden box under the seat. "Hey, Joe, here's a great big box. Ya reckon that's it?"

"Lemme see." Hualapai Joe dismounted, walked over, and looked inside the coach. "Maybe so. If we're lucky, that'll be enough for us to get outta Arizona Territory before the sheriff catches up with us."

Wedged under the seat, the box lid wouldn't open so they could check the contents.

Joe waved his gun at the passengers. "You three go pull that box out from under the seat."

The two men and the woman tried but couldn't budge it.

Grumbling, Joe and the third outlaw, Jack Benton, went to lend some muscle. Benton stood only five foot six, thin-bodied, and wasn't much help. The five of them still couldn't budge it.

"Git down here, Johnny. You're gonna have

to help," Joe said.

So Johnny climbed down. Even with his additional strength, they barely managed to slide it to the stage door. It tumbled out of the coach, falling like a huge boulder to the ground. Lefty pried the lid open and Joe lit a match. The glitter of gold sparkled from within.

"Holy Jehosephat!" Joe breathed. He had to use two hands to pick up one of the heavy ingots, but he soon dropped it because it weighed so much.

"I can't believe it," Benton exclaimed. "We're rich!"

Joe's match went out, burning his fingers. He shook them and scowled. "Yeah, but how're we gonna take it with us?"

Not wanting any witnesses, the bandits walked thirty feet away and held a whispered conference.

"Maybe we can drag it with our horses," Lefty suggested.

Joe disagreed. "Our horses ain't gonna last very long pulling that much weight."

"We can at least drag it far enough away so we can bury it without *them* watching us." Benton nodded toward Johnny and the passengers.

"Yeah," Lefty said. "We gotta do that."

"We're gonna have to find a few horses, or better yet, some mules," Joe said.

SHORT STORY MYSTERIES

"Or a wagon," Lefty added.

"No way around it." Joe scratched his head. "We're gonna have to bury the gold 'til we can git back."

"We'd better git Johnny and the passengers outta sight so they can't see where we're gonna bury it," Lefty said.

"Maybe we oughta kill 'em." Benton pulled his hat down over his forehead.

"Naw, we'll send 'em on to Needles," Joe decided. "Then we can go to the stage stop and steal some mules and a wagon."

Benton walked back and told the passengers, "Git those watches outta yur pockets and let's have yur money while yur at it." He and Lefty collected the valuables.

"Now git back in the stage," Joe ordered.

Thankful they hadn't been shot, the passengers scrambled inside. Johnny climbed up, yelled, and brought the whip down on the horses' backs. Startled, the horses leaped forward, and in his haste, Johnny dropped the reins. The team stampeded and the stage disappeared into the starry night.

The thieves didn't have a shovel, but wanted to get the heavy box out of sight in case something unexpected happened to delay their return, so they tied their lassos to the handles on the heavy box and dallied the other ends to their saddle horns. After dragging it a short distance away, they used their hands to dig a hole in the sand. They scooped plenty of sand over and around the box to cover it, mounted and headed for the last changing station.

Unbeknownst to the gang, someone had robbed an accommodation bank in a store at Mineral Park. The five-man posse thought Joe and his two coherts had done the deed and was hot on their trail. The posse rode to the Beale Springs station where the attendants told them that Joe and his two cronies had been there and left, so the posse rode on to the first changing station.

Reaching their destination just after sundown, the members of the posse unsaddled their horses and ate a meal. Strolling outside the weather-warped, wooden building for some fresh air, they saw three men riding in. The sheriff, Charlie Story, recognized Hualapai Joe as he tied his horse to a post and said, "Joe, you're under arrest."

Still in their saddles, the other two henchmen reached for their weapons and posse members shot them.

Joe tried to draw his six gun and Charlie Story fired, fatally wounding him. The lawmen carried the outlaw to the porch floor of the old building. Still breathing, Joe began to mutter.

Charlie bent to unstrap Joes's cartridge belt, felt a big lump, and pulled out a small sack of gold. A member of the posse found another one on Lefty. Each little sack had been tagged with the business owner's name, consigned to Los Angeles.

Someone brought a bottle of whiskey and the sheriff poured some in Joe's mouth.

"Where'd you boys get the sacks of gold?" Charlie asked.

"I'm a goner, ain't I?" Joe asked hoarsely.

"Right along with your pards who're already dead."

"Them sacks came off the stage Johnny Jump-up was drivin'."

"That stage carried a lot of valuables. You got the box?"

"Too heavy. Had to stash it. I was going back for it tonight with mules."

More whiskey kept the outlaw talking.

"We saw those guys load the box at Mineral Park and figured it was fulla gold. We were ridin' outta Arizona Territory when we saw the stage comin' down the road so we ambushed it. We like to never got that gold offa the stage, it weighed so much."

He gasped for air. "We robbed Johnny

Jump-Up and the passengers of their wallets and watches too."

One of the posse men ran to search the bodies and discovered the personal items stuffed inside the other two outlaws' shirts.

Joe continued. "The horses ran off, headed toward Needles. I could hear Johnny yelling at the teams and the wheels crackin' against the rocks." He drew a labored breath. "We broke open the box and didn't know what to do with so much weight. Then all at once I couldn't hear the stage wheels or Johnny yellin' no more."

"I looked up towards the distant road," he said, wheezing. "A bright starlit night, but nowhere could I see the stage. It just disappeared. Sheriff, it vanished into nowhere! You never seen so much gold and bags of money as was in that box." His voice trailed off into an incoherent mumble as he sucked in his last breath.

The next morning the posse buried the three outlaws a quarter mile from the station. They tried to recover the strong box by following the stage tracks but found only those made by a later stage.

Someone rode into Beale Springs two days later and asked why Johnny Jump-up's stage hadn't arrived in Needles.

The posse rode south again and searched all the way to the Southern Pacific Bridge on the

SHORT STORY MYSTERIES

Colorado but couldn't find anything.

I stopped the story at this point when I entered it in the Idaho Writers' League competition because they have a 2,500 word limit on creative nonfiction entries. But this tale didn't actually end here. Bobby and I were both intrigued with what transpired next.

No trace of the coach, passengers, horses, or gold ever surfaced —for sixty years.

Then in the 1930's, a mysterious man named Max Borden entered the picture. He had a craggy face and faded blue eyes surrounded by crow's feet. Those eyes seemed to see beyond distant horizons. He wore Levi's, a blue hickory shirt, laced boots, and a red bandana around his neck. His black Stetson hat always looked half-way worn out. Surprisingly, Max had good personal hygiene and his clothing always appeared to be clean.

Standing five foot nine, strong and well muscled, he never spoke much louder than a whisper. He was a nondescript person who could fade into the background so no one really noticed him. People would see him and then be unable to describe him. Nobody knew anything about his past or where he came from because he kept to himself. Most people considered him a hermit.

Max spent most of his life roaming northwestern Mojave County, especially in the sun-blackened Cerbat and Black Mountains and the desert around them, only coming to town two or three times a year. The local inhabitants labeled him an old man when they first realized he existed.

Maurice Kildare, a writer/historian, couldn't remember exactly when he first met Borden. "It probably happened in Kingman at the end of World War I," he said. "When prohibition ended, we'd exchange a few words in the Frontier Saloon." Few words were spoken because Borden didn't have much to say. Usually Kildare drank a Coke and Borden would drink from one to three beers but never more than that.

Sitting in Black's Bar in Flagstaff one September day in 1936, Borden surprised Kildare by asking a question. "Do you happen to know about a stage robbery south of Beale Springs in 1880? The stage and everybody with it was never seen again. It disappeared completely." He took a sip of beer. "First heard about it before 1900 and plenty afterwards."

"Let's go to my office and pull out some files," Kildare replied.

Sure enough, the story of Johnny Jump-up

SHORT STORY MYSTERIES

and the stage robbery by Hualapai Joe and his two cronies were documented in the files of clippings.

When Maurice finished reading the clippings, Borden cleared his throat. "The one thing I want to know, was there actually a heap of valuables in the strong box?"

"Let's go see Ace Harris in Kingman," Maurice replied. "He was around when all this happened."

Driving into Kingman, Max said suddenly, "Let me off here and *you* talk to Harris. It'll be better if you don't tell him anything about me."

Kildare pulled over. He was not surprised; Borden just didn't want to be involved with people.

Ace Harris had come to Beale Springs from Oregon in 1871 with his father. They had run cattle, and later Ace had worked 12 years as a county deputy sheriff.

The genial, big man wanted to visit for awhile, but finally Kildare got a chance to mention the stage robbery. Harris turned serious and related the story much the same as Maurice had read it to Borden. Maurice asked how much treasure was likely to be in the strong box if found.

After cogitating, Harris replied, "I'd say the most that could have been crammed into the box would run a little over two hundred thousand."

Maurice picked Borden up and related what the ex-sheriff's deputy had said. Max seemed satisfied.

In September, 1940, Kildare ran into Borden on the final day of the Kingman Rodeo.

"Take me back to Yucca," the prospector said. "Got something to show you."

Climbing in Kildare's black, 1939 Ford coupe, they drove to Yucca, located twenty-six miles south of Kingman, and arrived at Max's Sacramento Valley camp in late afternoon. That night, quite uncharacteristically, he reminisced about his mountain and desert experiences and of the countless times he had watched sunsets from the Black and Cerbat Mountains. How he loved them!

But the next morning Borden had reverted to his usual taciturn self. For nearly two hours they rode through the endless sandy spaces on two of the burros, the third trailing behind. Borden finally halted, dismounted and turned to Kildare.

"I'm figuring what I'm going to show you will not be mentioned. Not now while I'm alive. Don't want to be called a ghoul."

"Shucks, you been digging into aboriginal graves for ancient pottery?" Kildare laughed.

But Borden didn't smile. "No, you'll see why in a minute."

While standing there, the writer noticed the

far but shallow bank of a wide wash. The bank on their side stood approximately forty feet high. Back four feet from the rim, a deep, widening crack parted the surface. It was a dangerous fissure.

Going to a solid part of the wash rim, Borden pointed south. "What do you think of that?"

"The sight proved astounding," Kildare later wrote. "The off side of a stagecoach and the wheels showed barely clear of dirt, gravel and sand. Beyond the front end were whitened horse bones and black hardened bits of harness leather."

Much had been washed away during seasonal floods. However, digging around it had exposed the stagecoach. Removed debris had been shoveled back into the trench as it lengthened.

"That is how come the stage disappeared like the outlaw claimed," Borden explained. "It plunged over into this deep wash. The high bank must have given way with it, tumbled in on top, covering the whole shebang."

He paused, tipped his hat back. "Couldn't find no bones of Johnny Jump-up, though. Must of washed on down with the bones of the leaders (the lead team of horses.) Bones of the passengers are inside the coach but there isn't anything else in it."

"We should report this to the sheriff," Kildare said.

"Not me," Max objected in the next instant. "I want no palavering with nobody over this. Let someone else find and report it. But they better hurry. That crack is widening all the time. It'll plunge on down to cover the stage again for maybe another twenty to forty years."

As Kildare prepared to leave camp, Borden said, "I know you figure I ain't doing right, but from my side of it, there'd be too much confusion and publicity. A lot of hawnyocks would come around looking for that strong box filled with gold. Let it lie, doggo, and when I'm dead, you report it to the sheriff."

The writer said later he "couldn't begin to find that place again."

Then World War II intervened and four years later when Kildare began looking for the prospector, no one could remember when they'd last seen him. He never saw Borden again.

At last, convinced that Max had died in the mountains he loved so much, Kildare told the county sheriff about the buried stage that had disappeare in 1880, but the sheriff wasn't interested.

Max Borden and Maurice Kildare are reportedly the only people who may have seen or heard of the mysterious stagecoach or Johnny Jump-up since it disappeared. And no one has ever reported finding the $200,000 in money and gold ingots.

SHORT STORY MYSTERIES

Over the years, I've witnessed some horrible, almost unbelievable, abuses of horses. Many times, I've thought it a crying shame that the horse couldn't retaliate and extract revenge. In this fictional story, the lady horse whisperer works in reverse.

Strike Four, You're Dead

    Selma Atwood rode the three year old Palomino Quarter Horse colt around the Kernes indoor arena that lay next to the desert between Shoshone and Gooding, Idaho. Big posts were located at intervals along the arena walls. The artificial neon lights that hung on the rafters couldn't illuminate the interior quite as well as the sunshine lit up the outdoors. This was the Palomino's first time with a person on his back and he felt rigid beneath her, eyeing every shadowy nook and cranny. She let him take his time, checking out everything.

Suddenly, a tall, brown haired man wearing a blue plaid shirt and Levis jumped out from behind the roping chutes waving his black Stetson at her and the Palomino. The guy unnerved Selma, but he scared the colt out of his gourd. The youngster leaped four feet into the air and his back formed a perfect arc. He lit stiff-legged, jarring Selma's whole body. The petite, twenty nine year old horse trainer didn't want to yank on the colt's head at this early stage in training, so she left him alone for a few seconds. She had no trouble riding him; he had a smooth way of moving that felt like a fluid drive. Since the Palomino didn't happen to be a natural bucker, after two or three good jumps, he threw up his head and quit.

That guy deliberately provoked the colt into blowing the plug, Selma thought. *He tried to get me bucked off. That's strike one against you, stranger.*

The incident set her afire, for two reasons. First, she didn't want a colt to develop the habit of bucking. Second, she was a horse trainer, and even if she could ride a bad one, sooner or later one might get lucky and pile her. She didn't want to take that chance. Her two boys, eight and ten, depended upon her; she couldn't afford to be laid up.

She continued to ride the Palomino until he

quieted down, then she carefully dismounted. Slipping the halter over the colt's head, she tied him to a post, and stormed across the arena toward the stranger. Strands of dark hair had come loose from her pony tail during the bronc ride and the stragglers hung down below her baseball cap. Her brown eyes smoked with fury.

The man stood leaning against a post, a grin plastered on his face. Selma yelled at him from twenty feet away. "Just what in the hell do you think you're doing?" She came to a halt three feet in front of him and jammed her hands on her hips.

Still grinning, he gave her an insolent once-over from head to toe and back up. "Who me? I didn't do anything."

"That's a lie and we both know it. Did it ever occur to you that I don't want my colts to get in the habit of bucking?" If only she were a man! She'd wipe that hideous grin off his mug with a well-placed left hook.

"Why not? It don't hurt 'em." He turned away from her, then said over his shoulder, "You wouldn't have stayed with him if he hadn't stopped bucking." He walked on out into the alleyway.

Frustrated because she hadn't been able to vent the full force of her rage, she spun around, plodded back across the sandy arena and untied the palomino. Selma's sympathy lay with the horse. He'd only bucked because he'd been scared. If she'd been a colt, most likely she'd have responded in the same way.

Like most horse whisperers, she possessed the uncanny talent of being able to put herself in the horse's place and this ability made her a darned good trainer. Since a horse couldn't talk, trying to figure out what he was thinking often created a huge challenge, requiring much concentration and utilization of psychological principles. Not only did she have to decipher what the horse was thinking, but *why*. What had happened in a horse's past that had caused a terrible habit to develop? Why did he react to certain stimuli? And most importantly, how could she persuade him to lose the bad habit? As she conquered the challenges, she'd grown to enjoy the equine companionship much more than she did that of most human beings.

"Come on, fella, we'll go unsaddle and feed you." She stroked his neck. The Palomino colt was far enough along in training that she could hold him by a rein and unsaddle at her tack room door. She loosened the cinch, lugged the heavy Macpherson saddle just inside the door and swung it over a sawhorse, then led the colt outside into the bright sunlight and turned him loose in his pen.

Who is that guy anyway? she wondered.

SHORT STORY MYSTERIES

And why is he here? This evening after I finish riding my training horses, I'm going to talk to Sam Kernes about this yahoo. I don't want my training horses frightened that way. Drawing herself up to her full five foot four inches, she marched to her blue Ford pickup, hopped in and headed for home.

Selma always wore Lees, filling them out with a figure for which most movie stars would have died. During the week, she wore scuffed Tony Lamas, faded Lees and an old tooled belt with her name on the back in tarnished silver letters. But when she dressed for the horse shows, she looked as though she'd just stepped out of a western wear catalog. She was stunning with her diamond-shaped, silver-conchoed dark brown belt and matching spur straps that held her antique Garcia blued-steel/silver spurs in place. A whole month's wages had gone into the purchase of her alligator boots.

The single mother pulled into the driveway of her neat, but modest home, and hurried inside. She smiled at her mother who always came over from next door to watch the kids while she went out to feed the horses. Standing in the bedroom doorway, Selma lovingly watched her boys while they slept. They were good kids. Both had inherited her complexion and dark brown hair, but they were going to be tall like their father.

"Rise and shine, fellas," she finally told them.

As usual, Mark, the older, grumbled as he climbed out of bed; Gage, the younger, got up in a daze and stumbled down the hall to the bathroom while she headed for the kitchen to cook breakfast.

Ten minutes later, the boys came in and sat down just as she set their plates of bacon and eggs on the table. Both were half asleep and didn't have much to say until she spoke to them.

"Will you guys help Grandma today? She wants you to paint her porch," Selma said.

"Yeah, we'll help with the painting," Mark promised.

"And I don't want any arguments between you, okay? That upsets her." Hearing no response, Selma glanced up at them.

Grudgingly, Gage said, "Yeah, but tell Mark to leave my ball alone. He takes it away from me and then won't give it back."

Selma admonished Mark to leave Gage's ball alone. She didn't know if the boys would manage to keep the second promise, but her mother always called if the boys fought over something. Selma didn't want to have to quit riding a colt and go to town to settle an argument.

After dropping the boys off at Grandma's

house, she headed back to the arena thinking, *I'm so fortunate. I love what I do. Every day I can hardly wait to saddle my first colt and I can also earn enough money to support my boys. What more could I ask from life?*

She parked by the pens, haltered a chestnut, and saddled him. Sensing that he had become bored with riding in the arena, she gave him a respite by heading out across the desert. The colt threw up his head, and with his ears pricked forward, fell into a lively walk, checking out the new territory. She made a mental note to contact a neighbor who lived close to the arena to see if she could drive one of his calves around in his corral. If this colt had "cow sense", he'd take to the work like a duck to water, learning to rein as Selma signaled him to turn with the cow. By the time she made it back, the colt had been three miles and loved every minute of the adventurous cross-country ride. She unsaddled and turned him loose.

A bay colt was next on her list. She caught and led him to the tack room, then slid the saddle on his back. The bay didn't have much of a "handle" on him, so she rode him in the arena and worked him on basic maneuvers. After walking, trotting, and loping him, she gently pulled on the reins, asking him to come to a halt. She let him take his time, first slowing to a trot, then walking down to a stop. She asked for several slow turns, never applying any pressure so he became excited. He turned much better than he ever had before, so she immediately climbed off and loosened the cinch. Most likely he'd remember that he'd been rewarded for turning correctly and would do it even better the next time.

She started for the alleyway to go to the tack room and heard someone call her name. The old grizzled rancher/arena owner, Sam Kernes, stood beside the stranger who had scared her colt that morning. Sam wore a grin, gestured with his hands and laughed. The tall dork (at least she considered him a dork) laughed too. Selma wisely decided she'd better keep her cool until she found out what was going on.

Kernes tipped his misshaped, natural-colored straw hat back on his head.

"Selma, I'd like you to meet Russ Telford. Russ, Selma Atwood," he said. "Selma trains horses too. Does pretty good for a girl."

Selma couldn't let that go by without a retort. "For a girl? Give me a break, Sam!"

"I've never seen a woman who could train a horse yet," Telford commented. He didn't look at Selma when he said it.

"Well, you have now." She glared at him.

"She's pretty firey too." Sam laughed at her outburst. "Russ is from San Jose, California. He bought the Martin place down the road and will be training horses in this arena too."

Oh, boy, this is going to get interesting, Selma thought. Sam wants the extra income so he isn't going to listen to any gripes I have about this guy. I'll just have to make the best of it.

As soon as she could, she excused herself and unsaddled the bay. He walked a few steps when she let him loose in the pen, then dropped and rolled. When he stood up, dust covered his body. He shook and dust flew, but a lot of it still showed on his coat. By the time she returned to the arena, Telford had gone.

At nine o'clock the next morning, she stood brushing the Palomino colt, making sure all the hair lay flat on his back so the saddle wouldn't cause any sores. Telford walked through the arena gate leading a beautiful sorrel and white Paint Horse.

Always an admirer of good horseflesh, Selma said, "Nice looking Paint." Her words slipped out before she even realized it.

"Just another ole pinto," he shrugged.

"He's a doll!" she exclaimed. "And he has excellent muscled stock horse conformation which had to come from Quarter and Paint Horse ancestry.

In fact, that's why when the Paint Horse Association was formed, the founders limited the breeds included to Quarter Horses, Thoroughbreds, or other Paints—so the progeny would have good muscled conformation."

She realized she'd gotten carried away with her tirade. Telford turned away, signifying that he really didn't give a damn. Selma's brown eyes sparked at the snub.

Then the Paint Horse drew her attention. His eyes were wild and he sashayed nervously as Telford stuck his foot in the stirrup and swung into the saddle.

But Selma wasn't finished. "On the other hand, the Pinto Horse Association of America will register a horse from any breed as long as the horse has the pinto color."

Telford looked at her as if she had bats in the upstairs belfry.

"Look, he's definitely got stock horse conformation," Selma said. "No doubt he has papers. What breed is he registered with?"

"You don't ride the papers," Telford said smugly. "I threw those sonsabitches away."

"You what!" Selma couldn't believe anyone could be so ignorant. She immediately thought of the bumper sticker that said, "You can't fix stupid." Most people were *proud* of their horses and their bloodlines. With the horse's photo affixed to them, the papers provided proof, not only of background lineage for several generations, but in many cases, proof of ownership. *That's strike two,* she thought. *This guy's a blitherin' idiot.*

Without another word, Telford slashed the reins down across the Paint's hip and the horse leaped through the gate and toward the desert.

The realization hit Selma. This dork doesn't really like horses. Boy, is he in the wrong business.

She saddled the Palomino colt, led him outside, and mounted. Already a quarter mile away, Telford had headed northeast, the Paint prancing and flinging his head. Not wanting to follow him, Selma rode in a northwesterly direction instead.

It was a nippy but beautiful late April morning with a few fluffy white cumulus clouds floating lazily across the azure sky. The bright orange sun peeped above the mountains in the east, its rays slowly warming the earth. The sparse green desert grass struggled for life among the rock outcroppings and small clumps of violet, yellow and white desert flowers sporadically dotted the landscape. Even the usually dreary sagebrush appeared a brighter blue-gray in the early morning.

The Palomino had never been ridden outside the arena. His ears pricked forward and his steps were light, watching for any movement that might threaten danger.

"You've spent the last two years in your familiar, peaceful pasture and now everything is new and strange," Selma consoled him, realizing he was poised for flight, yet intrigued by the new surroundings.

He nickered nervously and a couple of sympathetic horses back at the corrals answered.

"Your buddies aren't going to save you, fella." She stroked his neck to lessen his fears and bolster his confidence. "But I'll take good care of you and you'll learn to trust me." The colt flicked his ears at the sound of her voice and the touch of her hand. "The world as you knew it has fallen apart now that you have to work for a living, hasn't it?"

Almost under the colt's nose, a pheasant suddenly exploded upward. Startled, the horse leaped into the air, folded, and propelled himself in the opposite direction. If Selma hadn't been an accomplished rider, he'd have lost her, but she stuck to him like a burr, and regained control.

"You're a quick little guy," she observed. "Not very brave but you're sure athletic!" She touched him on the neck again to reassure him and insisted he turn back in his same steps. "We'll ride outside every day so you get used to all the new scary things," she said.

In the next quarter mile, the Palomino tried twice to return to the other horses. Each time Selma gently, but firmly, kept him headed to the northwest.

"No, I'm the boss," she told him patiently. "We're going in this direction."

Unsuccessful in his attempts to return to his buddies, the colt eventually gave up and lined out.

She'd ridden about two miles up a ravine when she spied a flash of sorrel and white. Leaping and plunging, the Paint had refused to come down the hill into the ravine. Mercilessly, Telford began to spur, yet restraining the horse with a tight rein.

Is this guy nuts? If you want a horse to go forward, you give him his head. You don't hold him up.

Selma stopped the Palomino colt who promptly threw up his head and nickered at the Paint, but the sorrel and white was so terrified, he didn't answer. Rage contorted Telford's face as he drew blood with the wicked spurs. By reining in the horse, he didn't give the Paint a chance to respond. Selma, who constantly studied methods to gain the desired responses of her four-legged students, was always meticulously fair with her training and she couldn't believe anyone could be so cruel. Telford yanked and spurred relentlessly until the Paint finally sank to his knees, begging for relief from the pain.

"What do you think you're doing?" Selma screamed. Propelling the colt forward, she galloped toward Telford. She succeeded in diverting the man's attention from the pathetic creature that struggled to its feet and stood spraddle-legged, globs of foamy sweat falling from its belly.

"I'm teachin' him a lesson," Telford yelled back. "Mind your own damn business."

"You're not teaching him anything," Selma retorted. "All you're doing is punishing him—for no reason." At least, she sure hadn't seen the horse commit any unpardonable sin.

"Keep your nose where it belongs." He sent a hateful, arrogant look her way. "You're nothing but a hick from the sticks. You don't know shit about training a horse."

"And you think you do?" His so-called training methods were inconceivable to her.

"Damned right I do." Telford yanked on the reins to reverse the Paint, which had to bruise the horse's mouth. "I've worked with some of the best trainers in the business."

The Paint stumbled as he attempted to respond, but he had no energy left. Foamy blood dripped from his mouth. It made Selma sick.

Telford headed the beaten animal back over the hill. *That does it! There goes strike three,* Selma thought resolutely.

She herself valued each horse for its ability, its quirks, its individual personality. Although humans were not physically as large, they were supposedly superior in intelligence and, therefore, possessed the ability to dominate horses. They could come up with methods to induce a response to their wishes. Selma knew the Paint could have already reached the point of no return; he might never make a decent saddle horse after all the abuse he'd suffered.

She seethed, hating Telford for treating such a beautiful animal as he had. *It's too bad the poor horse can't fight back,* she thought. *He should buck Telford off. That would serve the bastard right. That Paint deserves to get revenge... And that idiot had the audacity to say I don't know how to train a horse! He doesn't know me—or what I can or can't do.*

Contemplating, she rode the colt another quarter of a mile before turning back, primarily because she didn't want to run into the sadistic, self-proclaimed "trainer" again, at least not that day. She couldn't stand the sight of him.

Three days later she encountered the dork

again and that morning's episode convinced her she had to do *something*. She'd saddled the bay colt and led him in the arena. On the far side, she saw the Paint tied low to a post, his head whipping from side to side, trying to escape as Telford beat him over the head with a big board.

Selma screamed, "Quit that, you sonofabitch!" Dropping the bay's reins, she ran toward Telford, not stopping to consider what she'd do when she reached him; she only knew she had to save the Paint from the hideous abuse.

The louse paused, turned toward her, a wild look in his eyes and beads of sweat dripping from his face from the exertion he had expended.

"Who does this horse belong to?" she demanded. "I'm going to let the owner know what you're doing to this beautiful animal." She didn't add that she also meant to talk to the Humane Society.

"*I* own him," he stated emphatically. "I can do whatever I damn well please with him."

Selma stopped short. *This sadistic bastard owns the gelding and he's using the poor horse as an outlet to vent his anger, just like a wife-beater. The horse is helpless, completely at this guy's mercy. That's definitely strike four! I've got to figure out how to stop this guy.*

Frustration rocked her. After all, there were

laws that protected animals against such treatment. Wheeling, she stormed out, drove straight home and called the Humane Society. A woman answered.

"I want to report a case of horse abuse," she said. "That man shouldn't be allowed near a horse, or any animal for that matter."

"Did you see him mistreat a horse?"

"I sure did," Selma stated.

"Where did this happen?"

"At the Kearnes arena west of town," Selma replied. "There's a so-called trainer there named Russ Telford. The other day he jerked and spurred his horse until the poor thing finally dropped to his knees. It was awful."

"You'll need to come into the office and file a formal complaint."

"I will, with pleasure." Which Selma did.

A small, plain-looking woman in black slacks and three-inch black patent heels sat behind her big oak desk and scanned the complaint. "I'll go out to the Kearnes arena right after lunch. No one should be allowed to mistreat an animal," she said.

Anxious to see what had happened between Telford and the Humane Society woman, Selma returned to the training facility by one o'clock. A gray, late model Buick sat parked beside the front door. Selma opened the door and peeked in. Telford was smiling, talking to the plain woman who now wore a black, hip-length leather coat. The woman raised her foot, pulling the high heel out of the sand. Head tipped back, her laugh echoed across the enclosure.

Selma's heart hit bottom. *Oh, no, he's sweet talking that fickle woman. She doesn't care about that poor, helpless horse. I can't depend upon the Humane Society to put a stop to the abuse.*

Sure enough, as the woman turned to go back to her car, Selma heard her say, "I'll see you Friday night, Russ."

"Dressed to the hilt, about eight o'clock," he promised with a sickly smile.

Venom is dripping from his mouth. Oooh, he makes me sick, Selma fumed. *I've got to stop him somehow, but what can I do?* She unsaddled her steed, turned him loose, and climbed into her pickup. She drove around for half an hour and just contemplated.

Telford says I can't train a horse but I know I can train a horse to do most anything. All it takes is time and patience. Oh, I wish the Paint would dump him. That would serve him right. That poor Paint may never be a calm, responsive riding horse, but I'd like to see him get revenge against Telford. So how can I train the Paint to buck the dork off?

She thought about Pavlov's experiment with the dogs and her eyes gleamed as an idea began to form. *Can't train a horse huh? We'll see about that!*

She drove the thirty-five miles to PetSmart in Twin Falls, selected and paid for a high frequency dog training whistle, the kind humans can't hear. Horses have acute hearing, and she was betting they could hear this type of whistle. Eager to put her plan into effect, she headed for home.

Early Saturday morning, she worked her colts in the arena, but left the Palomino saddled in a stall, hidden from view. Telford didn't show until ten a.m., looking like a truck had run over him. Selma peeked around the stall door, watched him saddle the Paint and slip his foot in the stirrup to mount. The horse shied, jumped away, and Telford didn't make it aboard. Selma quickly grabbed the dog whistle that she'd tied to a string around her neck and blew it. Telford slashed at the horse's shoulder with the reins. As the reins landed, Selma blew another short blast on the whistle. Afraid he was going to get lambasted again, the Paint panicked and ran backwards. Selma blew the whistle again. When Telford caught up with the spotted horse, he grabbed an ear and bent it in half, which is extremely painful, then he mounted.

Selma blew another forceful blast.

For three weeks, she followed Telford, always staying out of sight and watching. The horse began throwing more and more fits with every ride and each time, she blew the whistle. Disgust at the treatment of the horse made her want to just shoot the bastard. Telford didn't spot her.

One day the self-proclaimed trainer headed for the desert and Selma got a chance to test her theory. She followed, staying out of sight behind the rolling desert hills. As Telford started through a large outcropping of jagged, lava rocks, she saw her opportunity. She grabbed the whistle and blew a forceful blast.

The Paint dived forward, bogged his head, and kicked up his heels at the same time. He'd progressed to the point that he constantly threw fits, but he'd never really bucked in earnest before. He caught Telford unawares, and the jerk lurched too far forward. The horse leaped upwards, twisted, and turned his belly skyward, throwing his rider off balance. Taking two more jumps, the Paint sent the sadistic man sailing headfirst into a large pile of lava rocks. The sorrel and white spun in a blur and ran for the comfort and safety of his stall, gaining altitude with every stride as he ran by Selma and the Palomino.

Excited by the Paint's performance, her

yellow colt tried to run too. "It's okay, my baby," Selma said, stroking his neck and calming him. She watched the Paint as he raced over the hills, still bucking sporadically when the notion seized him.

Selma didn't approach the broken form lying among the rocks; she didn't want her tracks to lead anywhere near the victim. With a big smile, she headed the Palomino for the arena to retrieve and unsaddle the Paint. Before too long, she'd probably be able to buy him for a paltry amount and she'd have a chance to retrain the horse using patience and TLC.

LOY ANN BELL

Bobby Jones and Taylor Brown decided to enter the wild cow milking contest at Filer one year. The ending as Bobby told it really happened; however, the rest of the story is pure fiction. Sitting on my horse at the end of the arena, I watched the whole episode and I also happened to be driving when the four of us went through the fair gate. Those days were some of the most memorable and fun-filled in my life.

THE WILD COW MILKING CONTEST

One day in mid-August, 1966, Bobby Jones stopped at Barney Heideman's Saddle Shop to buy a new cinch. The six foot one, light brown haired cowboy from Filer, Idaho had cowboyed, roped, and trained Quarter Horses all his life and could tell "big windies" better than anyone around.

He spotted a flyer hanging on the bulletin board near the front door. It read, "Wild Cow Milking Contest." A jackpot with a $20 entry fee, $8 to pay for the use of the cows and $12 to be added to the purse. The event would be held at six o'clock Monday, September 5th, before the Twin Falls County Rodeo. Local cowboys welcome.

"Hey, I want to get in that," Bobby said.

"Think you can catch one of those cows?"

Bobby looked around.

Barney, the store owner, wore a big grin on his face. "Remember what happened a month ago at Gooding?"

Bobby remembered all right. How could he forget? "Yeah, I had a bad day," he muttered.

Barney laughed, not just a tee-hee, but a big belly laugh.

"You ran that poor old cow 'til she gave out and fell down. Then you rode over and dropped your loop over her head."

"I got her, didn't I?" Bobby growled. Personally, he didn't think it was all that funny.

Barney could hardly stand up straight. "Yeah, but she refused to get up and you finally turned her loose."

"Too much time had elapsed. I couldn't win any money, so I figured I might as well quit," Bobby said defensively.

A good two minutes passed before Barney regained his composure. "Who you gonna get for a partner if you get in this?" He nodded toward the flyer.

"I dunno. Haven't had time to think about

SHORT STORY MYSTERIES

it."

The partner would be the "mugger" and it took a strong person to handle that job. Figuring and studying, Bobby thought of several men but crossed each off his mental list.

"Have you thought about George Dalton?" Heideman asked.

"Naw, he's too bigga wuss. If a cow looked at him sideways, he'd run." Bobby paused. "Hey, I know who I'm gonna get—Taylor Brown."

Twenty-one year old Taylor stood six-one, stout as a bull.

Barney nodded. "Yeah, he could do the job."

Bobby ran into Taylor two days later. "Hey, they're gonna have a wild cow milking this year at the fair. Wanna get in it with me? I'll rope'er and you mug'er."

"Yeah, we can do that," Taylor replied.

Evidently he hasn't heard about the Gooding fiasco or he'd say something. Bobby let out a breath of relief. *Hope nobody ever tells him.*

"That'll be right down our alley, Jones," Taylor said, getting enthused.

"Think you can handle a waspy old cow?"

"Listen, I grew up on a ranch, wrestled, played football, bulldogged, and wrangled horses and cows all my life." Taylor grinned. "I shouldn't have any problem handling one measly old cow."

"Maybe," Bobby said doubtfully. "But lots of things can happen in a wild cow milking."

"Aw, if we plan our strategy down to the last detail, we can win the thing." Confidence oozed from the cocky young man.

Excited and apprehensive about the event, they paid their entry fees the next day. They didn't expect to get rich, but they sure wanted the prestige of winning.

They rehearsed and re-rehearsed every move they intended to make in the contest. Bobby planned to run his horse to the herd of cows and rope one. By the time he dallied his rope around the saddle horn, Taylor, on foot, would grab the cow's neck with one arm and her nose with the other hand and stop the wild cow. Carrying a little milk bottle, Bobby would bale off the horse. While Taylor held the bovine in place (much easier said than done!), Bobby would reach under the bucking, kicking cow and milk two or three squirts in the bottle (no easy feat either.) Then he would sprint for the finish line. They went over the plan until they had these moves down to a fine science; they meant to win the event.

A few days later, Bobby again stopped at the Saddle Shop, this time to buy a new shirt.

Heideman smiled at him. "Al Gorman's going to enter the wild cow milking too," he said.

"Oh, no," Jones moaned.

Five-eight, substantially built, and fun loving, Al could rope all right, but his roping ability wasn't the problem. Bobby knew the man all too well. Al liked to *cheat*. Whatever the contest, the conniving little rat always managed to cheat. It didn't even bother him if he got caught cheating. He just laughed about it.

"And he's helping with the contest 'cause he knows where he can get some cows," Barney said. "Getting the cattle might have been quite a problem."

Bobby sat back on his heels and figured and studied. He considered every angle, but finally decided there was no way possible Al could cheat on this one. *Whoever gets milk in his bottle and makes it across the finish line first will win,* Bobby thought. *There's no way that little twerp can rig this event. It's just that simple. Taylor and I can beat him. We will beat him.*

Barney's voice snapped Jones out of his reverie. "Dick Everton's muggin' for 'im." Bobby pictured Dick Everton in his mind. Tall, dark-haired, and substantially built, the man could ride, rope, and he was athletic.

"We can beat 'em," Bobby said with more confidence than he felt.

Fretting and stewing, he and Taylor waited impatiently during the two and half weeks until the rodeo.

For years, Twin Falls County has held its fair and rodeo in Filer for several days around Labor Day. FFA, 4-H, Mule, All-breed, Paint and Quarter Horse shows offer entertainment for contestants and spectators alike. Home-grown produce, jams, jellies, quilts, and hand-sewn garments are judged for top honors, the winning ribbons displayed on them in the merchant buildings. A bustling, noisy carnival attracts kids of all ages. Vendors rent booths to sell jewelry, hot dogs, hamburgers, Mexican food, and delicious fudge. Businessmen and women sell hot tubs, cars, trailers, and water purification systems. It's a bustling place involving the whole Magic Valley. Excitement charges the air.

Enthusiasm spills over to the rodeo too. A well-known rodeo contractor furnishes top-notch bucking stock, good capable clowns keep the crowd entertained, and the show runs smoothly, one event after the other.

Wednesday finally arrived. Bobby, a buddy, and their wives pulled up—late and in a rush—to the fairgrounds gate with Bobby's horse in the trailer. A gateman, a badge pinned to his shirt, bravely, but foolishly, stepped out in front of the pickup. The delusional man had been given authority, probably for the first time in his life. The buddy's wife who was driving started to stop. Knowing they'd be detained at least ten minutes, Bobby hollered, "Run over the son of a bitch!" The buddy's wife did as Bobby instructed and kept driving. Thankfully, at the last minute, the gateman jumped back.

An adrenaline rush hit Bobby when he viewed all the activity. Then he remembered the Gooding rodeo when he couldn't catch the cow and doubts assailed him. He didn't want to let Taylor down, but he couldn't help but wonder if he could rope a cow quickly enough for them to win the wild cow milking.

Taylor walked up just as Jones unloaded his roan gelding. "Ya ready for this?"

"As ready as I'll ever be." Bobby quickly brushed the hair flat on his gelding's back, slapped the saddle on, and pulled the cinch tight. "Let's warm up the horses."

"Meet ya at the gate." Taylor headed for his trailer where his horse stood tied.

They rode around the arena until the announcer's voice boomed, "The first contest of the evening is the wild cow milking. When they call this wild cow milking, they ain't kiddin', folks. This event can get rough!"

A cowboy opened the south gate and twenty five head of frenzied Hereford cows streamed into the arena. One old cow lowered her head and chased the gateman, blowing snot in his hind pocket until the man leaped for the fence, and scurried up and over it like a monkey.

These cows are total idiots, Bobby thought. They're running in every direction as if they're a flock of quail that somebody spooked.

"Bunch them together," the announcer instructed.

Several cowboys tried to shove the cows into a group, but being wild, range bovines, the cows had no intentions of cooperating. One charged, knocking a horse flat, and sending its rider sprawling. The men became slightly more cautious.

The white-faced cows darted everywhere. The announcer finally lost his patience and called, "Ropers, line up."

Bobby stood his roan behind the starting line along with the other contestants.

When the whistle blew, he jumped his big gelding toward the closest cow, outrunning the thundering horses behind him. His loop settled over her head, and Bobby dallied his rope around the saddle horn. Her bag looked full enough to contain milk (a minor but essential detail.) She began bellering and fighting the rope. The big roan braced himself to stop the cow from pulling him over.

Cows scattered in every direction as the riders descended upon them. Bobby concentrated on keeping his horse from being rammed by horns or run over by stampeding stock. Horses collided with one another, cows bawled, and riders fell off.

Bobby couldn't help but grin as the cowboy beside him lit headfirst in a fresh cow pie when his horse stopped suddenly. All green and yucky, the man sputtered and spit as he pulled himself out of the mess. The crowd loved it.

One cowboy yelled, "That big ole cow just stomped on one of my new Tony Lama boots!"

"Hey, some of these cows are dry. They don't have milk!" someone else hollered.

Another roper fell off his horse and an angry cow dived at him. She hooked a horn under his belt. The belt broke with a loud pop. The guy tried to run from the rampant bovine, but he couldn't, 'cause his pants had fallen down around his ankles, hobbling him. He really looked macho crawling around on his hands and knees, his fanny in the air, little red hearts plastered all over his boxer shorts. The cow hit him on his heart-covered butt and sent him flying. He resembled a spread eagle before he lit face-first in the dirt. The crowd roared.

One cowboy had changed his mind about mugging the cow and kept trying to go in the opposite direction. But he couldn't; he kept moving with a funny, sideways gait. Bobby noticed the cowboy had skinny, bird legs and he'd poked his pant legs down into his fancy, colorful boot tops like the Texans do. His cow, a small one, had somehow managed to step into his right boot. Every time the man took a step with his free leg, the cow dragged him back by his other leg and butted him. The contestant's face had a surprised look, as if he couldn't figure out what was happening. He hollered for help, but nobody paid any attention; they had their own problems.

Bobby jerked his mind back to his task.

A terrified Hereford raced across the roan's path and plowed headfirst into the woven-wire on the bottom part of the arena fence next to the announcer's stand. Out of the corner of his eye, Bobby saw Dick Everton hightail over and grab her before she could get her head free. Al Gorman charged his horse toward Dick, nearly running over two mounted cowboys.

Dick is supposed to rope the cow, Bobby thought, not catch one trapped in the fence. Guess Al found the right partner, one that doesn't mind cheating too.

Bobby dragged his struggling cow in his mugger's direction, while Taylor ran as fast as he could toward them. As the young cowboy reached out to grab her, the cow swung her head and hooked him with a two-and-a-half-inch horn. The blow hit him in the ribs and completely knocked the air from his lungs. Taylor lit on his belly with a loud "whoof!" and began gasping for air.

Bobby groaned. *We're done for now. My partner's got the wind knocked out of him.*

But Taylor was no quitter. By sheer willpower and determination, he regained his feet and stumbled after the cow. As she leaped around on the end of Bobby's rope, Taylor reached out and latched onto her. Bobby noticed the bellering cow seemed to bounce around more than she should have. Then he saw why. Taylor's eyes were nearly smoking, he was so furious. The cow had hurt him and he'd retaliated. He had the cow's ear in his mouth, biting as hard as he could. Blood flowed from the red hairy ear.

No wonder that old cow is bawling. I'd bawl too if Taylor was chewing on my ear.

But Jones didn't have time to worry about their cow. He baled off his gelding, ran to her udder and, bending over, tried to avoid the flying feet. She kicked him twice, and stomped on his big toe before he managed to milk three or four squirts into the little bottle. He stood up, started to run, then stopped. He didn't know which way to go. Where was the finish line? Scanning the chaotic scene, he realized he and Taylor had finished well ahead of the other competitors. Finally, he spotted the judge standing in front of the grandstand.

Ducking and dodging, Bobby headed in that direction. "Hey!" he yelled, trying to attract the man's attention, but the judge was looking the other way and couldn't hear above the cacophony of bawling cows, neighing horses, and shouting cowboys. Bobby came to a screeching halt beside the man, nearly knocking him over.

"I got milk. See?" Bobby held up the bottle so the judge could see the dab of white liquid. "We win, right?"

"No, the finish line is over there!" The judge pointed toward the north gate beside the calf roping chute.

Bobby scanned the arena. No one else had any milk in a bottle yet and they wouldn't know where the finish line was either. He still had time. Desperately trying to avoid being killed on the way, he ran as hard as he could for the gate.

Then he spied Al Gorman taking a bottle out of his shirt pocket, white milk already showing in the bottom. Al didn't look toward the judge or hesitate for a moment, but ran for the finish line. And he was closer to the gate than Bobby!

That darned Al knew where the finish line was. He put the judge in front of the grandstand on purpose so everybody would run the wrong way. And damn the cheatin' little SOB, he's gonna win. Despite his short legs, I've never been able to outrun him.

Fueled by adrenalin, Bobby gave it his all, picking his feet up and laying them down as hard and fast as he could. But no matter how badly he wanted to, Bobby couldn't catch the little ratfink.

Al crossed the finish line first. Furious at being beaten, Bobby was even madder at being outmaneuvered. He should have known Al would manage to cheat somehow.

"That darned Al knew where to go," Bobby complained to Taylor afterward. "I know he told the judge to stand by the grandstand so everyone would think that's where the finish line was."

"I'll tell you what else Al did," his young partner said. "He never even got close to that cow. He already had milk in his bottle."

"I saw that. He's such a …a…!" Bobby sputtered. He couldn't think of a word bad enough to describe Al.

Taylor nodded in agreement. "He sure is."

* * *

Ten years later, while searching for a tee shirt in his dresser drawer, Bobby discovered the uncashed second place check where he'd stuffed it under his clothes. It was for the huge amount of $11.00. The priceless, irreplaceable memories all came flooding back of how Al had outfoxed him in the wild cow milking contest.

Anger again surged through Bobby as he picked up the check. "Damn that dirty, little cheatin' so and so anyway!" he muttered.

Stymied" placed in the 2011 IWL Adult Genre Fiction Category.

STYMIED

I recognized their voices, talking and laughing, in the next alleyway as soon as I stepped into the big barn located next to the Sawtooth National Forest in southern Idaho. Two years of marriage hadn't dulled Jarrett and Kit Fullmer's intrigue or enchantment with one another. Contrary to most couples in the horse business, a mild competition only seemed to keep their marriage more interesting.

"You watch, "Painted Hills" is going to win the Idaho Pleasure Horse Futurity," Kit said in a teasing voice.

"Naw, he's a nice horse, honey, but he isn't going to win. "Makin Music" is. That's 'cause I'm ridin' him," Jarrett responded.

"'Cause you're riding him?" Kit laughed, a pleasant, tinkling sound like chimes rustling in the wind. "He's a nice horse, handsome, but Painted Hills has a better way of going."

"You wouldn't wanna bet on that, would you, lady?"

"Of course, but what kind of stakes are we talking here?"

"Well, they should be high enough to make it worthwhile."

I could visualize him grinning at her.

"Okay, if I win," Kit said, "you take me out to dinner at Maddox's in Brigham City. Then I get whatever I want in bed that night."

A feeling of envy swept over me. Kit turned heads wherever she went, whether she wore her Wranglers or three inch high heels with a snazzy cocktail dress. Her long glowing hair she kept frosted; her emerald eyes sparkled with life; and her five foot five body was slender, yet curvy. She also had a fun loving, magnetic personality, and always seemed to say the right thing at the right time. I liked her, really liked her. Too much.

But I could see what had attracted her to

Jarrett. Six feet two, he had broad shoulders, blond, wavy hair, and a captivating grin. They made an impressive, attractive couple and I wondered if he realized how lucky he was.

Jerrett said, "But if I win, you have to treat *me* to dinner at Maddox's. And I get whatever I want that night."

"Deal!" She laughed.

What I wouldn't have given to have been in his boots right then! I'd have conceded the win or my soul to her. She could have had whatever she wanted *every* night.

Snapping back to the real world, I stepped around the corner and surprised them in a passionate kiss.

My face felt hot and I knew it had turned crimson. "Hi, you two," I said, feeling like a rat for thinking the envious thoughts I harbored for her. I'd fallen more than a little in love with my friend's wife, for hell's sake! Fallen enough in love that I hadn't even looked at another woman for at least six months. I knew the mental street I was traveling could only lead to a dead end, but couldn't seem to help myself.

They pulled apart as if captured in a wrongdoing. Jarrett looked like a cat caught playing with a canary, but recovered quickly and grinned at me.

Kit laughed at my discomfort. "It's okay. We're married."

"We're arguing over which of us is going to win the Idaho Pleasure Horse Futurity," Jarrett said, which I knew to be just a half truth. "I hope one of us does anyway, 'cause the owners of both horses we're training said we can keep our winnings. There are enough horses entered, it should pay at least $2,000 for first place."

"Two thousand dollars, huh?" I also needed to be a little more concerned about the money because my contract with the owner of the black and white Paint I was riding stated I could keep whatever I won too.

Kit grabbed a halter from the tack room, disappeared into Painted Hills's stall and came out leading the pretty brown and white pinto mare. A registered Paint, the mare showed the muscled conformation desired by the American Paint Horse Association (APHA), resulting from a three-breed infusion of Quarter Horses, Thoroughbreds, and other Paints.

Jarrett and I caught our horses and we all saddled up. We followed as Kit led the mare down the alleyway to the arena that joined the huge barn on the east. Tightening her cinch, she mounted, and squeezed her legs to cue the mare to walk. Kit sat erect, legs straight with her hips in line with her ankle bones. She possessed light hands that didn't hurt a horse's soft, pliable mouth.

Technically, we competed against one another since all three of us were in the horse training business, and when we entered the arena gate at a show, we did our best to win. But we were also comrades, good friends. If I won, they were first to congratulate me; if either of them won, I did the same.

We schooled our western pleasure futurity horses, then put our other training horses through their routines.

Jarrett's third horse was a stud named "A Diamond in Colors." "Colors" was, by nature, cantankerous, and acted worse than usual that day. He totally refused to turn to the left, sulling, and finally leaping in the air when Jarrett gigged him with a spur to alter his mindset. I'll admit studs can be stubborn, but I was amazed when Jarrett's face turned purple with rage. It's common knowledge among good horsemen that "you can't teach a horse anything when you lose your temper." Showing no mercy, Jarrett began jerking on Color's mouth and spurring him, leaving red peeled-up patches on the horse's shoulders.

I'd known the man for two years and had no clue that he possessed such a violent temper. He fought with Color for fifteen minutes straight. The horse's coat turned white and frothy sweat dripped from his belly. Jarrett had passed the point where he could teach the horse anything; he'd only wanted to hurt, to punish. Hating to witness the abuse, I sucked in my breath, then exhaled slowly when the horse finally gave in and turned to the left. It took Jarrett awhile to cool down and his face to lose its cruel expression.

The last horse Jarrett rode that day was "Docs Special", a gorgeous black and white Paint stud. "Doc", as they nicknamed him, was a grandson of Doc Bar, a Quarter Horse who founded the greatest dynasty of cutting horses the world has ever seen. Jarrett and Kit owned Doc. The horse was a looker; he had a little "doll head" and his satiny coat gleamed when he moved. They had a right to be proud of him: he'd won points at halter where a horse is judged on its conformation, had won both the Idaho and Utah Western Pleasure Futurities for two year olds the preceding year and had acquired points at seven other events.

This year, Jarrett had begun cow cutting with Doc and the horse exhibited the athletic ability, cow sense, and intelligence to excel at this advanced event too. In fact, Jarrett had even started winning in the open cutting contests where the competition is tougher. As a result, the horse's

SHORT STORY MYSTERIES

worth had tripled. Jarrett and Kit planned to stand the horse at stud, but were wondering how to get the most out of their advertising dollars.

* * *

When I pulled into the fairgrounds at Filer the following weekend, people were hurrying every which way, some on foot, others leading or riding horses. Kit had mailed my entries with theirs so our horses would be stalled side by side. Fullmer's van sat empty in the parking area, disconnected from their horse trailer. I headed for the office and picked up my horses' numbers. Each horse is assigned its own number and show records are meticulously kept so points are attributed to the horse who won them. Then I walked into the barn to check things out before unloading.

Kit saw me, smiled and asked, "Want to go eat with us?"

"Sure," I replied.

Jarrett finished carrying buckets of water to the stalls and Kit spread the straw in my stalls ahead of me as I unloaded and put my horses away. Less than ten minutes later, we piled into their pickup and drove the six blocks to a local restaurant that someone in the barn had recommended. The someone had been right. We liked the down-home atmosphere and the food tasted wonderful.

Sleeping in the living quarters of our trailers had its advantages, because we could be close to the prize horses for which we were responsible. As I drifted off to sleep, I wondered whether Jerrett or Kit would win the bet regarding the futurity. They were both good trainers; one or both of them would surely place in it. A visual image of them lying in bed popped into my mind, and I blocked it out immediately. After all, Kit was not mine and I certainly had no right to covet her. Nor was it any of my business who won the bet.

The next afternoon, Kit won the trophy on Painted Hills; I won second, and Jarrett earned third place. Nearly bouncing with exuberance, Kit treated us both to a scrumptious dinner at the Sizzler in Twin Falls. Remembering their bet, I wasn't surprised when they asked me to check on their horses before I hit the sack that night so they could spend the night at a motel. I agreed, masking any indication as to how I really felt. How it hurt to think about their night of bliss.

The next morning I had just finished spraying the barn alleyway with a fine mist from the hose to keep the dust down when I noticed a black Mercedes B-Class creeping down the street. I figured the driver didn't want to dust up the showroom floor shine on the fancy car or he wanted to impress everyone with his $250,000 possession. Maybe both.

The car stopped in front of the barn, the door opened, and a pair of boots hit the ground that probably cost more than a couple of months' wages for a guy like me. When the man himself appeared, he surveyed the surroundings like someone always on the lookout for potential acquisitions. Dressed in a royal blue western suit and silver belly Stetson, he exuded confidence. This guy wasn't just a big frog in a puddle; he owned the whole lake.

He sauntered into the barn, found the banner proclaiming Jarrett and Kit's stable name, and stopped to view their horses. He stopped at Docs Special's stall and studied the horse for a few minutes before turning to me.

"Do you know where Kit Fullmer is?" he asked. "I need to talk to her while I'm in this part of the country."

"They should be back anytime," I replied.

Just then Kit and Jarrett walked in, laughing, arms around one another.

"This man wants to talk to you," I told them.

Jarrett didn't act as though he recognized the man, but Kit did. Approaching us, she exclaimed, "Carl! What a surprise," and hurried to give the stranger a quick hug. Turning to her husband, she said, "Jarrett, this is Carl Ashley. He's from Ft. Worth, Texas. I bought Docs Special from him when Doc was only 30 days old."

Surprised, I did the math: Doc was five now, so Kit had purchased the stud before she married Jarrett. Most likely Kit was still listed on the registration papers as Doc's owner.

Jarrett and Carl Ashley shook hands.

"I heard you got married," Ashley said to Kit, "I understand Doc is quite a performance horse. And he's doing great at cutting too."

"He is," Kit said. "We're so proud of him."

Ashley smiled. "Have I got a proposition for you! Is there someplace we can grab a cup of coffee and some breakfast?"

"There's a little café not far from here." Kit turned and introduced me, then asked, "You haven't eaten yet, have you? Why don't you come with us?"

A warm feeling surged through me at her invitation. "But if you're talking business…"

"Nonsense," she said, and turned to Ashley. "He's our best friend."

Ashley shrugged. If Kit wanted me along, it was all right with him. We walked out to his shiny Mercedes. "Sit up here with me, Kit." He opened the front passenger door for her and she hopped in while Jarrett and I climbed into the back seat.

At the restaurant, we ordered, and Carl Ashley stated his proposition, directing his pitch mainly to Kit. "My stallion station has grown," he said. "I now stand six horses--two are AAAT race horses, two are prize show horses, and one is a top-notch cutting horse by Smart Little Lena."

He took a sip of coffee. "I need a Doc Bar Paint horse to round out my roster. The colt you bought from me would fill that niche quite nicely. He's good looking, he's already acquired an enviable show record, and he's showing a lot of promise as a cutting horse."

"We're going to stand him here," Jarrett interjected.

"He'll get better quality mares from Texas and Oklahoma," Ashley pointed out, "especially the cutting horses. This is a real opportunity to build Doc's reputation."

Lines furrowed Kit's forehead as she considered the proposition.

"I've made the horse," Jarrett protested. "He wouldn't be worth a dime if it hadn't been for me."

"Well, you trained him," Ashley conceded, "but it's difficult to ruin a real good horse."

Jarrett didn't argue that point.

From that moment on, Kit's voice reflected

excitement anytime she talked. Ashley picked up the tab.

On the way back to the fairgrounds, he added another selling point. "I do a huge amount of advertising on the stallions I stand at the station and your horse will certainly benefit from the national coverage. You'll make a lot of money on this deal, but you will reap the benefits for years to come. Most people would grab the opportunity."

Kit nodded. "I know."

"Well, you think it over and let me know what you decide, but don't wait too long. I've got to start the advertising campaign within a month." He waved as he drove off.

Our horses needed to be shampooed and brushed, their manes and tails combed in preparation for that day's classes, so we hurried to get them ready. Afterward, we quick-changed into our show duds in our horse trailers.

I hardly caught a glimpse of Kit or Jarrett that day except when we passed one another going to or from the arena. On Sunday morning, we compared our winnings before we loaded up to head for home. On the way, I detoured to visit an old rancher friend, so Kit and Jarrett had dropped their horses off, fed and were gone by the time I arrived at the barn.

During the next couple of days four new

colts were dropped off for me to train that required extra time and attention. I had to start them "from scratch" in the round pen, familiarizing them with a rope around their feet, legs and everywhere else on their bodies, then finally saddling them. When I mounted each of them two days later, not one of the four gave me any problems. Because this process occupied my time, I didn't get a chance to talk to Kit or Jarrett.

At 10:15 Wednesday evening, I had dozed off in my easy chair when Jarrett called.

"Have you seen Kit?" he demanded.

"No," I answered, wondering if he'd guessed how I felt about Kit. Why else would he call *me*?

"She went to a meeting in Twin Falls tonight and she's not home yet. She's always back by now."

"Did you call someone who attended the meeting?"

"Yes. She never showed."

"Did she have her cell phone with her?"

"Yes. She doesn't answer."

"Did you call the police or the hospitals?"

"Yes. The police haven't heard anything and she's not in any of the local hospitals. The police won't take a missing person's report for twenty four hours, so I'm calling everyone I know. Someone must have seen her."

"Give me some names and I'll help you call."

He did and I jotted them down on the pad I kept by the phone, then called until I'd run through the list. The clock chimed midnight just as I finished the last call.

It took three attempts before I got through to Jarrett.

"No luck," I told him. "How 'bout you?"

"I'd have let you know," he said dejectedly. "I guess the next step is to drive to Twin Falls and make sure she's not stranded on the road somewhere."

"I'll go with you," I offered.

He picked me up within seven minutes. Five and a half miles away from their house, we found her Buick parked beside the road. The car was locked, but Jarrett had a car key on his key ring. When he opened the door and shined a flashlight beam over the interior, we could see no blood or any signs of violence indicating Kit had been forcefully abducted. Jarrett called the Sheriff's Department on his cell phone.

Thirty minutes passed before a deputy responded. Grabbing a flashlight, the deputy checked inside the car, but didn't see anything more suspicious than we had. Taking out a notebook, the deputy asked Jarrett and me a lot of questions that neither of us could answer. The deputy finally closed the notebook.

"Your wife probably had car trouble. Why don't you try starting the engine?"

Jarrett scooted into the driver's seat, inserted the ignition key and turned the switch. The engine fired up immediately.

"Your wife has probably just gone with a friend and will come home soon," the deputy said. "Please call us if she shows up, will you?"

Jarrett nodded and said he'd come and get the car in the morning. The deputy left and Jarrett dropped me at my house.

The clock said four a.m. when I went to bed, but sleep wouldn't come. After hearing the living room clock chime five times, I finally hopped up and dressed. Grabbing my cell phone and shoving it into the case attached to my belt, I headed for the barn and fed early. By 6:30, Jarrett hadn't shown, so I fed and watered his and Kit's horses too.

With no word, I nearly went crazy, so I kept busy by working with the new horses. Jarrett came dragging in at 5:30 that evening and I bombarded him with questions.

"No, no one's seen her," he said, his voice

full of anxiety. "I filled out a missing person's report and they're going to put it over the news tonight."

I nodded.

"The police questioned me for two hours. They act like I killed her, for hell's sake."

That didn't surprise me. Family members are always first on the suspect list, and I told him so.

"I loved her." He brushed at his eye. "We were crazy about one another. If they talk to you, you'll tell them, won't you?"

"Sure," I said.

"I'm so tired. Thanks for feeding my horses for me this morning." He climbed in his pickup and drove slowly out the driveway.

Devastated, I prayed that Kit would turn up, unscathed, her beautiful face wearing her gorgeous smile.

But she didn't. I never saw her again. She simply disappeared.

The police questioned me at length, but I couldn't help them.

Suspicions began forming in my mind when, within a month, Jarrett hired an attorney and legally became the agent for Docs Special. In other words, he acquired permission to stand the horse and collect the $2500 stud fee for each mare bred. Six months later, he finagled a court order to have the ownership of Docs Special transferred into his name. He also let it slip one day that, upon the death of her grandfather, Kit had inherited a sizeable oil dividend payment which was automatically deposited into their bank account each month.

"I'm sure glad Kit left a will naming me as the beneficiary," he remarked.

Over the next few months, I became more and more convinced that Jarrett had done away with his beautiful wife. They'd probably argued over who would stand the horse and he'd killed her. Most people hadn't witnessed his violent temper like I had.

My theory ate at me so intensely I finally drove to the sheriff's office and talked to Mort Staynor, the detective in charge. About fiftyish, Staynor looked fit and trim, as if he worked out two or three times a week. His brown suit was pressed and his geometric-figured yellow and brown tie showed good taste and careful selection.

"I think Jarrett killed her," I said bluntly, then told him about Carl Ashley's offer.

Staynor rocked back in his chair, contemplating. "Could be," he mused.

"Well, why don't you arrest him?" I asked.

"Oh, we think he did it all right," he said, "and we'd arrest him, but we can't."

"Why not?" I demanded.

"There are three things we need to build a case: one is motive; two is opportunity; and three is a body," Staynor said. "No doubt Jarrett had the opportunity, but, if she was murdered, we can't establish the time of death and check his whereabouts." He stared at me. "You've just provided us a motive, which we didn't have before. But without a corpus delicti, we're stymied. We can't prove a murder's been committed."

"I know he killed her," I insisted.

He leaned forward in his chair. It thumped when it hit the carpet. "There is a chance they had an argument and she just took off."

"But why would she do that?" I asked. "She could have divorced Jarrett. After all, she owned Special Doc; he wasn't community property."

Staynor shook his head. "We'd love to get him for murder, but without a body, we can't build a case."

I left, resolving to get the goods on Jarrett. For the next few months, I studied his every move, trying to figure where he'd hidden Kit's body. I think he felt my surveillance because his attitude toward me gradually changed.

One day he brought a twenty-two-year-old,

attractive redhead with him to the barn. The hero worship in her eyes was obvious when she gazed at Jarrett. She wanted to ride and show horses and he was her ticket to the glamorous horse world.

Sensing my repugnance, he caught me in the barn while the girl groomed a horse. "I don't intend to live without a woman," he told me. "I'm too young for that."

No words came to my mind and I just stared at him.

After a few minutes he took his protégé and left with her nearly sitting on his lap. Within a month, he moved to Montana with her, away from my prying eyes.

The thought has crossed my mind that Jarrett could have driven to the Great Salt Lake the night Kit disappeared and dumped her, alive or dead, with a big block of cement attached to her feet. But if her body is discovered, even twenty years from now, it's my hope that Jarrett will be convicted of the terrible crime I'm convinced he committed.

But so far justice hasn't prevailed and, just like the cops, I'm stymied.

LOY ANN BELL

This story is actually creative nonfiction. Bud Warren had a place in Perry, Oklahoma and owned more great Quarter Horses than any one man deserved. Bud definitely knew a good horse when he saw it.

MURDER, UNADULTERATED

Bud Warren of Perry, Oklahoma loved fast horses. He had an eye for top-notch Quarter Horses and a sixth-sense that told him which ones had the right genes to reproduce the speed traits.

He believed that to get blazing speed, the sire should be fast and the dam should have a good track record or at least come from speedy parents. Even then, regardless of parentage, most horses are not outstanding reproducers. Bud knew speed could be taken out of a bloodline faster than you could put it in.

LOY ANN BELL

In the mid-1940's, Warren started building a broodmare band and purchased his first registered Quarter Horse mares. One of these, "Swamp Angel", boasted excellent speed bloodlines and was in foal to a running horse called "Leo." In the spring, she had a filly that Bud named "Leota W." Bud liked the pretty little filly and when she proved to be fast on the track, he zeroed in on Leo for his breeding program.

A bright sorrel stallion with a wide blaze, Leo was foaled in 1940 and possessed a world of speed. He ran his first race when only 18 months of age and luckily stayed sound. By his third year, he'd run many races and won them. It soon became difficult to find people who hadn't heard of Leo's reputation; if they knew the horse, they seldom ran their horses against him. Unable to find races for him, Leo's owners would sell him. He changed hands so often that the registration transfer papers couldn't keep up with the ownerships.

One owner sent him into Mexico for match races where two horses are matched against one another, but Leo suffered an unfortunate trailer accident which caused injuries to both of his front legs, leaving his left knee permanently resembling a big stovepipe.

In 1947, the horse ran his last race for a purse of $1,000 in Tulsa. He gave it everything he had, but lost by a head, running down the stretch favoring his bad knee.

Bud called the American Quarter Horse Association (AQHA) to locate Leo's current owner and bought him. For the first time in his life, Leo found a permanent home. The horse had a beautiful disposition and soon became a member of the family, and because of his remarkable race record, he attracted well bred mares. Not only was the horse an outstanding individual, but he proved to be a prolific sire and when his offspring reached racing age, they began burning up the tracks.

Leota W became an outstanding racing filly, rating AAA, the fastest speed on the Quarter tracks. In the year-end awards presented to the fastest, most consistent running horses, Leota W was named the 1947 Co-Champion Quarter Running two-year-old. Another daughter, Miss Meyers, ran AAAT, the fastest time possible, and earned the dual titles of 1953 World Champion Quarter Running Mare and Horse. A son, Palleo Pete, ran AAAT, and became the 1954 Champion Quarter Running Stallion.

Soon Leo's influence extended beyond the racetrack. His sons and daughters won in halter, arena events, and cutting. Palleo Pete's full brother, Holey Sox, ran AA on the track and went on to become the 1963 NCHA (National Cutting Horse

Association) World Champion. Another son, Leo San, sired Wimpy Leo San, 1961 high-point halter horse and Leo San Van, 1961 high-point halter and cutting gelding in '61 and '62. Leo San also sired Peppy San, the 1967 NCHA World Champion and Mr. San Peppy, who won the title in 1974 and 1976. Both these Leo grandsons (full brothers) became outstanding sires.

Leo's daughters were fantastic broodmares. King's Pistol out of Flit was the 1957 NCHA World Champion. Leo's speedy grandget out of Leo dams included Vandy's Flash, World Champion Quarter Running Gelding in 1958 and 1960 and World Champion Quarter Running Horse in 1960. Vanetta Dee became World Champion Quarter Running Mare in 1956, '57, and '58; Vannevar was World Champion Quarter Running Gelding in 1956 and '57.

Bud, a true horseman, took great pride in his horses and felt as though he'd bought into a piece of heaven. He'd discovered one of the greatest, if not *the* greatest, sire in the AQHA.

Twenty years after his death, Leo's daughters were still leading the nation for having produced the most Quarter Horses to qualify in racing, arena performance, and at halter, a nearly unbelievable statistic.

Twenty four of Leo's sons and daughters

proved their versatility by winning AQHA Championships. (An AQHA Champion must earn a total of 35 points acquired in AQHA-approved halter, performance, or racing events. Further information can be found at www.AQHA.com, Member Services, Member Action, Handbook Show Rules, paragraph 425.) Leo also had one Supreme Champion, which requires a total of 40 points.

Leo established Bud Warren as an owner/breeder of top-notch Quarter Horses. Sires like Leo don't come along often, and Bud loved the horse. Even when Leo's daughters came to breeding age, Bud didn't sell him; instead he leased him to prominent breeders around the country.

Through the years, Bud owned many stallions, but when he talked about Leo, the intense emotional attachment showed.

"People thought I was crazy for buying a crippled stallion, but I had a hunch that horse would be a sire," he said.

Leo had a wonderful disposition and influenced the Quarter Horse industry tremendously. He stamped his offspring with color, conformation, and disposition.

"He put heart and try into them, and just like their daddy, most of them didn't know when to say quit," Bud said. "By the time the horse was twenty three, his old knee injury was causing a lot of trouble. It was getting bigger and bigger. We did everything we could, but we couldn't seem to slow down the calcium buildup.

"It reached a point that it was so bad, he'd get down and couldn't get up. We'd go out to the barn and help him, put bales of hay around him, anything we could do to help him get a little relief. He'd be on his feet a few days and then go down again. He was healthy in every other way, but the constant struggle with that knee literally wore him out.

"Then the day came when he got down and couldn't get up, even with our help. He tried as hard as he could. He knew he wasn't sick. He knew he didn't feel bad other than the pain of that knee. He struggled and struggled but it just wouldn't support him. He gave it everything he had."

Tears came to Bud's eyes as he remembered Leo's terrible battle.

"He tried so hard he was hurting himself. He kept hitting against the stall, bumping his head, bruising himself. We decided the only remaining kindness we could give him was to put him to sleep."

Bud brushed at the tears and glanced out the

window.

"He's resting on that hill across from the house, with a tombstone to mark the spot. Leo was about as good as they'll ever come."

The horse died in 1967. Leo had brought so much business to the town of Perry, Oklahoma that a city park was named after him and a statue of him erected.

* * *

There's a saying among horsemen: "a person is entitled to one good horse in his/her lifetime." With exceptional judgment and a whisp of luck, Bud Warren defied those odds.

He owned some great mares by Leo, and the Oklahoman wanted a top quality son of Three Bars to cross on those prized mares, infusing speed and more size, yet keeping stock horse, muscled conformation.

A Thoroughbred stallion, Three Bars had broken out of the starting gates fast and flew for five furlongs, which is slightly more than a quarter mile. Crossed on Quarter mares, the offspring were establishing their own reputations as good looking, blazing speedsters.

In 1953, Bud Warren stopped at Ken Fratis's place in Lemoore, California and spotted a Three Bars horse that he thought would be right for his

LOY ANN BELL

Leo daughters.

"I had walked down to the arena where they were working some cutting horses," Warren said. "One of the boys was holding herd on a good looking sorrel stallion which I judged to be about four or five, although I could tell he was awfully green. He had a good flat hip about a mile and a half long sticking out from under that stock saddle. And what a beautiful head! In fact, he was pure quality from head to tail."

When Bud asked about the horse, he was surprised to find the sorrel was a two-year-old son of Three Bars named "Sugar Bars." Bud had looked all over the U.S. for a quality colt by Three Bars, but hadn't found one that suited him until he saw Sugar Bars. He tried to buy the colt, but the owner didn't want to sell him, so Warren temporarily forgot about him.

In his freshman year on the track, Sugar Bars ran well enough, starting six times with three firsts, one second, and two thirds. There was nothing spectacular in his performances, however, and his owner decided to sell him. Roy Hittson of Imperial, California, purchased him. Sugar Bars started twenty three times as a three-year-old, with four firsts, two seconds, and six thirds. In his final race in 1954, at Phoenix, he qualified for his AAA rating.

SHORT STORY MYSTERIES

Bud Warren was somewhat perturbed when he heard the horse had been sold, but he didn't give up. Contacting several friends who knew the current owner, Bud asked them to let him know if the horse came up for sale again. One of those friends was AQHA inspector Bob Weimer and in January 1955, Warren received a call from the race barn in Tucson.

"It was the middle of the night," Bud recalled. "Hittson (who owned Sugar Bars) was in need of some cash and had instructed his trainer to sell Sugar Bars to the first person to show up with $2,500 in cash. I didn't have $2,500 in cash, and there were no banks open. To make things worse, it was Saturday night and nothing would be available until Monday.

"Bob said Hank Wiescamp (a prominent Quarter Horse breeder from Colorado) was interested in the horse, but he wanted to come down and look at him. John Hazelwood, who trained Leota W for me, was there in Tucson with Bob. He got on the phone and told me he had $2,500 stashed in his sock! He went over, bought Sugar Bars, and took him to his barn. I drove down with a trailer the next day and got him."

Sugar Bars possessed an air of independence. "When we unloaded him," Mrs.

Warren said, "he and Bud had an argument about manners right there on the spot. He was a hotheaded horse, but he learned some manners from Bud. Most of our horses would walk up to Bud and put their heads on his shoulder as soon as they saw him. Not Sugar though. He just wasn't the type to use anybody's shoulder."

Hugh Huntley, another of Bud's friends, observed, "Sugar Bars was a smart horse, but he was also mischievous. Many times I can remember putting a halter on him. He'd look me straight in the eye while I was doing it, acting as if he were so glad to see me. Then, quick as can be, he'd nip me."

Bud immediately retired Sugar Bars from the track and set him on a career at stud that few horses ever equaled. Foaled just a decade after the formation of the AQHA, Sugar Bars helped usher in a new era in the evolution of the Quarter Horse. Out of every conceivable kind of mare, he sired speedy, good-looking, athletic horses that could and would do whatever was asked of them. During each season that Bud stood him, as many outside mares had to be turned away as were booked.

Altogether, Sugar sired 867 registered foals: 148 of those earned 2,574 points at halter; 147 won 4,465 performance points in the horse show arena; his colts earned $378,081 on the race track, (no small sum during those early years); 9 won Superior Halter Awards; and 27 earned Superior Performance Awards.

Sugar Bars' sons also proved to be prolific sire Jewel's Leo Bar (known as "Freckles"), a 1962 colt out of Leo Pan by Leo, established a dynasty of cutting horses for Marion Flynt of Midland, Texas. Grandget and great grandget of Freckles are now scattered throughout the nation and are remarkable performance horses.

Sugar's daughters were just as potent as his sons. They produced 462 Register of Merit race horses who earned $2,490,028; 140 accumulated 2,714.5 points at halter; and 300 garnered 6,279.5 performance points.

Sugar sired 30 AQHA Champions.

Over the years, Bud turned down many offers to sell Sugar Bars, one for $50,000, a veritable fortune then. Finally, in 1968, he agreed to sell the sorrel stallion to Dean Parker of Utah and Sid Huntley of California.

"I had about 15 Sugar Bars' fillies and a number of his daughters in my broodmare band. I also had several Leo daughters who were out of Sugar Bars mares. This left me with only a half-dozen mares that I could breed to Sugar Bars without going to line-breeding.

LOY ANN BELL

"I'd stayed with the horse long enough. I figured he would have the opportunity to be crossed on a lot of good mares on the West Coast that would not have come to him in Oklahoma."

So Sugar Bars moved to California.

In June 1972, at the age of 21, Sugar Bars suffered an attack of colic. He underwent surgery at UC-Davis where a colon-blocking tumor was removed, but the horse couldn't recover. He died of heart failure.

* * *

In 1961, Bud Warren dropped by J.B. Chambers' place in Littleton, Colorado to see J.B.'s new acquisition—a long yearling named "Jet Deck." The bay stud colt was sired by Moon Deck, a prominent speed sire, and out of Miss Night Bar by Barred by Three Bars. Chambers had never seen the colt, but he'd seen his full sister, Miss Jet Deck, run and wrote a $6,500 check, the asking price for Jet Deck.

"Jay had a little 40-watt bulb up the top of that barn and we couldn't see nothing', but I thought I had seen all I wanted to anyway." Bud told Wilbur Stuchal, a trainer/friend, "If that's a race horse, I'm gonna quit the business."

A phone call from Stuchal the following spring, before Jet Deck had even started a race, gave Warren his first clue that he might have missed the mark in his assessment of the colt.

"I had nothing to do whatsoever with Jet Deck at that time, other than the fact that Wilbur had some of my colts in his stable along with the horse.

"Charlie Smith, the only jockey to ever ride Jet Deck, was working the colt on the track that morning, and another jockey was putting a blow in Tee Beau, a tough AAA stakes horse. Here comes ol' Tee Beau down the track with the jockey a hoopin' and hollerin', and before Charlie knows it, Jet Deck grabs the bit and, from almost a standing start, runs up and eye-balls ol' Tee."

"It scared Charlie to death because he knew Wilbur didn't want to work Jet Deck that fast, afraid he would hurt him. But Charlie and Wilbur knew what they had after that little episode, and Wilbur called me to let me know, so he could rub it in about the statement I had made up at Jay's."

Jet Deck won his first start at Bay Meadows in California on February 27, 1962, a 350-yard allowance on May 3rd, and the Juvenile Championship at Los Alamitos. Then he shin-bucked (which happens to a lot of race colts) and had to be laid off until fall. In October, he won the Juvenile Prep at Arizona Downs; in November, he won the Juvenile championship over his three-quarter brother, Top Moon, and equaled the two-year-old colt record of the day.

In December, 1962, he set the straightaways on fire by winning the Pacific Coast Quarter Horse Racing Association (PCQHRA) Cal-Bred Futurity, Los Alamitos Futurity, and the Kindergarten Futurity. In the latter, he set a two-year-old world record of 19.9 for 400 yards.

He finished the year with earnings of $138,341, the most money ever won by a two-year-old up to that time. In 1962, he was named the Champion Quarter Running Stallion and the Champion Quarter Running Two-Year-Old.

Jet Deck began his three-year-old campaign on January 5, 1963 at Bay Meadows and finished it on December 21 at Los Alamitos. In between he won the PCQHRA Derby, the Los Alamitos Championship, the Ruidoso Championship, the Rocky Mountain Quarter Horse Derby, and the Colorado Wonderland Championship, running AAA and AAAT (the top of the AAA rating) consistently. He became the first Quarter Horse to win over $200,000 and was named 1963 World Champion Quarter Running Horse, 1963 Champion Quarter Running Stallion, and 1963 Champion Quarter Running Three-Year-Old Colt.

Bud Warren watched Jet Deck's highly successful racing career. Of course, Chambers and

Stuchal never let him forget his initial remark about the horse and kidded him unmercifully.

One day at Ruidoso, Warren asked Chambers if he'd lease Jet Deck. Chambers liked the idea of Jet Deck standing at the home of Leo and Sugar Bars (and, of course, to Bud's mares that had been sired by them. What owner who wanted to promote his stallion wouldn't?) The two men shook hands to cement the deal and the bay horse went to Oklahoma to stand the 1964 season. In 1967, Warren managed to purchase a half interest in him.

Jet Deck's get were as great as he was an individual and set the tracks afire. By 1971 he was, at the young age of 11, a leading race horse sire who had barely tapped his potential. As much as 18 years remained in his breeding career; his get could be expected to win a great deal more money on the race track, and make a definite mark in the performance and halter classes also.

Bud, Chambers, and everyone else who bred to Jet Deck were making money, a lot of money. But the bay horse had earned more than Warren's respect as a sire; Warren loved the horse for his disposition and personality. The pride Bud felt for Jet Deck was similar to what he had felt for Leo.

On August 26, 1971, Jet Deck was found

dead in his paddock at the Warren Ranch, discovered by a long-time Warren employee at 7:00 a.m. when he arrived to do the morning chores. An extensive post-mortem examination revealed that Jet Deck had died of a massive injection of barbiturates into the jugular vein ("main lined.") The mystery of who killed the bay stallion remains unsolved.

Reba Warren, Bud's wife, remembered the legendary stallion well. "He was one of the most gentle horses I've ever been around," she recalled. "His gentleness was probably one of the reasons he was killed so easily. He probably gave the people who did it no trouble.

"He was extremely easy to handle as a stud, and he enjoyed as much attention as he could get. I can remember lots of times when people would come to the ranch to take pictures of him. He'd run and play for them, doing everything he could to help them get a good picture."

Stuchal said, "As a sire, he was the greatest...he had wonderful conformation, great desire and determination, and the best coordination of any horse I've ever seen in my life. There aren't enough words to describe his loss to the horse breeding industry."

After Jet Deck's death, Bud completely lost heart; he no longer had any interest in racing or the

SHORT STORY MYSTERIES

breeding program he'd spent his lifetime building. Buyers at the dispersal sale were shocked to find the precious daughters of Leo and Sugar Bars "empty", not in foal; they'd never been bred back. Nothing mattered to Bud anymore. He only marked time until he passed away on January 15, 1988, at the age of 77, his heart broken by the loss of the horse he loved so much.

It was murder, unadulterated murder.

I've heard two rumors through the years as to who might have given the horse the overdose. One man who owned a son of Jet Deck said, "The mafia couldn't outrun him, and they couldn't outrun his colts, so they killed him."

Later, I heard that a shirt-tail relative who didn't get along with Bud gave the horse the overdose of barbiturates.

Whoever did it not only robbed Bud of his will to live, but also the Quarter Horse industry of one of the greatest sires that ever existed.

LOY ANN BELL

ABOUT THE AUTHOR

Loy Ann has lived most of her life around the Twin Falls, Jerome, Idaho area. She began riding when she was two and a half, got her own horse for her fifth birthday and has ridden ever since. In high school, she belonged to the Jerome Square Dancers (on horses), became a rodeo queen several times, and showed Quarter Horses. She barrel raced at the rodeos and worked for Pacific Northwest rodeo producers.

She left home to train cutting horses and give riding lessons in southern California. Having access to the best trainers in the nation, she began writing and was published in eight U.S. horse magazines and one in England. During this time, she also started playing bass guitar and singing in a band. Returning home after nine years, she raised Quarter Horses and Paints and continued to write stories and play music.

The author is presently President of the Idaho Writers' League, Twin Falls Chapter. And is a past State President of the IWL.

Loy Ann has two daughters, three grandchildren, and one little great granddaughter. She resides in Jerome with her dog, two cats, and two horses.

Email her at lan_paints@yahoo.com